Inside/Outside is accompanied by a number of printable online support materials, designed to ensure this resource best supports your professional needs:

- Go to https://resourcecentre.routledge.com/speechmark and click on the cover of this book
- Answer the question prompt using your copy of the book to gain access to the online content

"I couldn't wait to start trying out Joe's ideas which take personal development beyond the classroom and make it possible to engage a wide range of learners for whom chalk, and talk is not their preferred modality. Joe's breadth, depth and clear 'how tos' make this book indispensable."

Pooky Knightsmith, Mental Health Ambassador and Educator

"There are so many fantastic ideas in *Inside/Outside* that Schools can implement and embed across all subjects in their Curriculum. Teachers can use these creative ideas with resources to instil the importance and benefits of learning outside in nature, helping to support, boost young people's health and wellbeing."

Edd Moore, Multi-Award Winning Primary School Teacher and Eco Coordinator

"Joe Harkness is a force of nature. Full stop. This book is a prerequisite read for any educationalist working within the complex world of emotional intelligence. By reliving his own experience, Joe forges a connection between the outdoors and positive learning experiences. From Maslow's hierarchy of needs to the ever more prevalent awareness of mental health, he challenges the reader to identify their own triggers to an emotional response. Joe uses a level of psychology to encourage a level of self-reflection that is seldom seen in education. He has opened my eyes. A must read."

Darren Hollingsworth, Principal, Cromer Academy

"They say, if you're lucky when you're at school, you'll have one teacher who will change your life. I was lucky. Mr Carnegie was an incredible teacher who, besides officially teaching me English in the classroom, outdoors kindled a lifelong love and appreciation of the natural world. Quite unnoticed by me at the time, he gave me the tools to be a better person, a more thoughtful and calmer young man. This was decades ago. How many people now are so fortunate to find such a teacher? Perhaps now, thanks to Joe Harkness, a great many more may do so. *Inside/Outside* is written with insight on so many levels – it is perceptive, intuitive, and shines with his love for the natural world and the power it contains for positive change."

Jon Dunn, Author of *Orchid Summer* and *The Glitter in the Green*

Inside/Outside

Inside/Outside is a unique educational resource for those working with young people of secondary school age, providing a variety of tried-and-tested indoor and outdoor lessons and activities to promote and embed emotional literacy.

The book is divided into three accessible sections: emotions and feelings; self and situation; and mental health and wellbeing. Each covers a variety of themes, from anxiety and depression, to happiness, communication, and confidence. For each theme, 'inside' and 'outside' activities are offered, with inside activities inspiring students to self-reflect and develop empathy for others, and those outside drawing heavily on nature and learning outside the classroom. The 'outside' activities are adaptable and have been designed to work in any available outdoor space, and all activities can be used either in standalone lessons or sequentially, with introductory tasks, group activities, independent tasks, and group discussions.

With a focus on equipping students with meaningful and tangible skills to support them in the recognition, identification, and expression of their emotions, *Inside/Outside* will be a valuable resource for teachers, youth workers, home educators and anyone else looking to facilitate nature connection and introspection in children aged 11 to 16.

Joe Harkness is a naturalist and SEND teacher from Norfolk, England, where he runs an autism base in a mainstream secondary school. In 2019, he wrote *Bird Therapy* (Unbound), which was longlisted for the Wainwright Prize the following year.

Inside/Outside

A Nature-Themed Resource Book for Embedding Emotional Literacy

Joe Harkness

Routledge
Taylor & Francis Group
LONDON AND NEW YORK

Cover image: © Lisa Dynan

First published 2024
by Routledge
4 Park Square, Milton Park, Abingdon, Oxon OX14 4RN

and by Routledge
605 Third Avenue, New York, NY 10158

Routledge is an imprint of the Taylor & Francis Group, an informa business

© 2024 Joe Harkness

The right of Joe Harkness to be identified as author of this work has been asserted in accordance with sections 77 and 78 of the Copyright, Designs and Patents Act 1988.

All rights reserved. The purchase of this copyright material confers the right on the purchasing institution to photocopy or download pages which bear the support material icon and a copyright line at the bottom of the page. No other parts of this book may be reprinted or reproduced or utilised in any form or by any electronic, mechanical, or other means, now known or hereafter invented, including photocopying and recording, or in any information storage or retrieval system, without permission in writing from the publishers.

Trademark notice: Product or corporate names may be trademarks or registered trademarks, and are used only for identification and explanation without intent to infringe.

British Library Cataloguing-in-Publication Data
A catalogue record for this book is available from the British Library

ISBN: 978-1-032-36443-8 (hbk)
ISBN: 978-1-032-36444-5 (pbk)
ISBN: 978-1-003-33198-8 (ebk)

DOI: 10.4324/9781003331988

Typeset in Avenir LT Std
by KnowledgeWorks Global Ltd.

Access the support material: https://resourcecentre.routledge.com/speechmark

Contents

Acknowledgements x

Introduction 1

What is emotional literacy? 1

Why emotional literacy? 3

Why outside? 4

How to use this book 7

Section 1: Feelings and emotions 11

What are feelings? 12

Sonic sit-spot 14

Regulating emotions 16

Counting birds 18

Self-care and coping 20

Design-a-duck 22

What do we need? 24

Natural colours 26

Fear and phobias 28

Counting insects 30

Contents

Anger	32
Sensory sit-spot	34
Happiness	36
Gratitude scavenger hunt	38
Section 2: Self and situation	**41**
Self-awareness	42
Texture bingo	44
Identity	46
Sense of place – street work	48
Conflict	50
Our habitats	52
Communication	54
Mindfulness in nature – birdsong	56
SWOT analysis	58
Signs of sustainability	60
Respect	62
Counting wildflowers	64
Friendships	66
Bling up a butterfly	68

Section 3: Mental health and wellbeing	**71**
What is mental health?	72
Have-a-go-at-haiku	74
Poor mental health	76
The A–Z of noticing nature	78
Depression	80
Nest building	82
Anxiety	84
Nature mandalas	86
OCD	88
Fashion a feather	90
Stress	92
Regulation – outdoors	94
An active mind	96
Nature calm jars	98
References	*100*
Appendices	*103*
Index	*133*

Acknowledgements

Thank you to my wife, Emma, for once again putting up with me saying this was finished when it really wasn't and to my beautiful daughters – I do all this for you. Thank you to every school I've worked in that has allowed me to develop my teaching in PSHE and emotional literacy, particularly Future Education in Norwich, which timetabled it as a once-weekly subject for all form groups. Special mention for the Wolves who were my guinea pig class and to Rachel and Kirsty for running the sessions properly with their forms. This book is for the handful of teachers who tried to support me when I had given up on myself, Nigel Youngman, Iain Mackintosh and Simon Derrick, especially. You all shaped me as a teacher, and an author, more than you will ever know.

Sometimes you must fail to then rebuild and succeed.

Introduction

What is emotional literacy?

Who better to ask than the young people you work with themselves? When I first introduce the idea of emotional literacy to my own students, I ask them what they generally think the term might mean. I encourage them to break it down into two words and try to tease a loose definition out of them. They tend to get bogged down into defining the word *literacy*, which draws immediate connotations with its literal meaning of the ability to read and write. However, further down in the listed dictionary designations of the word is the one I seek from my students and that is to have knowledge, skills, and capabilities in a particular field or area, in this instance, our emotions.

You could find that this definition resonates with the other name for emotional literacy you may be familiar with, emotional intelligence, which was coined by Claude Steiner back in 1979 (Coppock, 2007). The notion of us being able to be emotionally intelligent came about in 1990, over a decade after the coining of the term emotional literacy. Research sets clear parameters between the two terms, with emotional literacy being defined as a *practice* and emotional intelligence as an acquirable *ability*. To give this an educational slant, emotional literacy is the formative process by which one achieves the summative outcome of emotional intelligence; and thus, it is evident that an emotional literacy intervention must be practically applicable in its facilitation. Others have also called it *emotional competency*, which also lends to the idea of a measurable attainable ability model.

Emotional intelligence can be defined as 'the accurate appraisal and expression of emotions in oneself and others and the regulation of emotion in a way that enhances living' (Mayer et al., 1990). Or to summarise – recognising our own and other people's emotions and learning how to regulate them. Most of the research into this field focuses on 'self' and 'other' as key themes, meaning that any work with young people around emotional literacy must focus on both them and the people around them in equal

Introduction

measure, both acting as a catalyst to considering the more refined areas that make up emotional literacy and intelligence.

There is also a useful table in the book *Nurturing Emotional Literacy* (Sharp, 2007), which compares the frequency of various elements of emotional literacy, and it is through studying this and a range of models on what makes us emotionally literate that I have identified five core strands to use as the framework for any intervention:

- self-awareness
- empathy
- self-regulation
- relationships
- motivation.

If you think about all the young people you have encountered over the years, especially in a professional context, it is probably fair to say that all of them struggle with at least one of these areas; and most likely several of them. As educators and professionals, we are in a privileged position to be able to teach and support young people to develop and nurture these skills, whether intentionally or not. It is difficult to define emotional literacy in the context we work in, however, through the depth of research I have looked at, I consider that it must, in a broad sense, serve to *focus on equipping our students with the skills and understanding needed to support them in the recognition, identification, management, and expression of their emotions.* This will be the ethos underpinning this book.

Much of emotional literacy explores what you may recognise as the 'social skills' identified in the old SEAL (Social and Emotional Aspects of Learning) framework (Humphrey et al., 2010) and my five core areas are all underpinned by this. In a social context, Bruce specifies the importance of creating a 'specific space' for an emotional literacy intervention, both physically and metaphorically (Bruce, 2010). The DfE adds to this in its guidance on compulsory health education (DfE, 2019), stating that schools should engender an atmosphere that encourages openness; ultimately forming the 'positive learning environment' defined by Cherniss et al. (2006). This focus on a mentally healthy environment is also one of the eight principles that Public Health England and the DfE (DfE and Public Health England, 2021) outline for promoting a whole-school or college approach to mental health and wellbeing. Simply, we cannot promote emotional literacy if we do not provide the right environment in which to nurture it.

Why emotional literacy?

The simple answer is that it is part of our statutory requirements as educators and those who work with young people, however vulnerable or disadvantaged they may be. As was just mentioned, in 2021 the Department for Education (DfE) introduced compulsory health education for both primary and secondary-age students. The accompanying statutory guidance states that both age ranges should be taught explicitly about physical health and mental wellbeing as part of their school curriculum. We are told that as educators, we must specifically promote our student's self-control and ability to self-regulate (which we know to be essential components of emotional literacy). We are also told that we should be directly working to reduce stigma attached to health issues; and particularly those regarding mental health. Therefore, as part of teaching young people to be able to recognise emotions, we should ground their fundamental knowledge of what poor mental health may look and feel like for other people around them as well.

The statutory guidance also outlines several specific content areas that young people should have been taught before the end of secondary school. I have tried to weave these key themes into the 'inside' activities of this book:

- How to talk about their emotions accurately and sensitively, using appropriate vocabulary.
- That happiness is linked to being connected to others.
- How to recognise the early signs of mental wellbeing concerns.
- Common types of mental ill health (e.g., anxiety and depression).
- How to critically evaluate when something they do or are involved in has a positive or negative effect on their own or others' mental health.

Furthermore, and perhaps most importantly given the context of this book, the guidance states that we should teach young people about the benefits and importance of time spent outdoors, for our mental wellbeing and happiness.

Prior to this, in 2018, the DfE released a guidance paper entitled 'Mental Health and Behaviour in Schools'. This describes how schools can implement a whole-school approach

Introduction

to mental health, explores the intrinsic link between mental health and behaviour in schools, and tells us that schools play a central role in enabling their students to be resilient (DfE, 2018). The following year, the Office for Standards in Education, Children's Services and Skills (OFSTED) updated its school inspection framework to include a deeper scrutiny of pupil personal development in school, focusing on several areas, including confidence, resilience, and mental health – areas which we know form part of the core of emotional literacy.

As we recover from the COVID-19 pandemic, the mental health and wellbeing of our young people has never been more important. Some have missed huge swathes of their in-school education, not to mention the social and emotional engagement that they experienced there. Many were thrust further into an online world, where, for some, all interactions, academically and socially, occurred in a virtual environment. In a January 2021 survey, UK youth mental health charity Young Minds found that young people aged 13–25 were most concerned about loneliness, isolation, and breaks in their education. In fact, 67% of those surveyed believed that the pandemic would have a long-term negative effect on their mental health (Young Minds, 2021).

What are the real-world applications and impacts of improved emotional literacy? In 2006, Cherniss et al. identified some real-world successes that could be attributed to emotional literacy, including 'effective leadership and workplace performance', and in a 2005 meta-analysis of school-based emotional literacy programs (Durlak et al., 2011), improvements in attitude, academic attainment, and prosocial behaviours, as well as reductions in conduct and the internalisation of problems, were also noted. This is further supported by the work of Weare and Gray (2003), who cite increased inclusion, greater social cohesion, and improvements to overall mental health as positive impacts. More succinctly, the Mental Health Foundation states that there is 'strong evidence to support connection between emotional literacy skills and mental health in children and adolescents' (Mental Health Foundation, 2019). Simply, an intervention *at any school age* could potentially generate positive societal outcomes in the future.

Why outside?

Outdoor learning takes on many guises. The most recognised must be Forest schools, but what about Guides and Scouts? When I went to Scouts as a teenager, most of our learning took place outside and was based around experience and skills development. Biology and geography curriculums still feature what we could call 'fieldwork', and many schools still facilitate field trips; all of which are forms of outdoor learning. Then there are approaches that utilise outdoor spaces for agricultural and/or horticultural purposes, such as care farming and school allotments. When I was at school, the more affluent students often went on extravagant field trips, which could be defined as 'adventure' or 'expedition' learning experiences. The point I am trying to make is that there are many ways to learn outside and lots of these are happening in schools all the time, but just because we encourage young people to learn outside, does it mean that they really appreciate the outdoors?

Richard Louv, eminent author of *Last Child in the Woods* coined the term 'nature deficit disorder', or NDD, to define young people's increasing alienation from the natural world, and the effects that this can have. I have always been dumbfounded by a 2002 study that found that 8-year-olds were more likely to be able to identify Pokémon characters than common British wildlife species (Balmford, 2002). While naming and categorising natural things is not detrimental to enjoying the outdoors, it could be argued that holding a foundation knowledge allows you to appreciate things more. That said, as we know that outdoor learning takes many forms, recognising and identifying specific details of natural things would perhaps not be as relevant in an adventure-type activity, for example. Whatever the approach, a recent systematic review of nature-specific outdoor learning on school children's learning and development categorically found that 'nature-specific outdoor learning has measurable socio-emotional, academic and wellbeing benefits.' It also recommended that it should be part of every young person's school experience with explicit reference to their local context (Mann et al., 2022).

When writing my book *Bird Therapy*, I undertook extensive research into the wellbeing benefits of being outdoors. One of the standout papers was a report titled 'Natural Thinking', which was written in 2007 for the Royal Society for the Protection of Birds (RSPB) (Bird, 2007). Its subtitle outlines what its purpose was, namely investigating the links between the natural environment, biodiversity, and mental health. I won't deconstruct it in depth here and instead will list some of its key findings and recommendations relating to the purpose of this book:

- Between the ages of 13 and 17, there is a reduction in affinity for a natural environment.
- Adults who spent time outdoors as a child are much more likely to show pro-environmental behaviours and revisit green spaces as an adult.

Introduction

- Parental anxiety and negative media portrayal can impact access to and connections with nature.
- Some studies show that children's ability to 'concentrate and be more self-disciplined' can improve with contact to nearby nature, such as a view of a green space.
- Outdoor activities appear to lessen the symptoms of attention deficit and hyperactivity disorders (ADHD).
- Exposure to nature can relieve the symptoms of stress for young people and help to improve self-esteem.
- The government should encourage schools to reconnect children to the natural environment.

With increased recognition of the wellbeing benefits of being outside and evidence that young people are much less engaged with outdoor interests, there can only be a logical negative correlation between the two; which in our privileged position working with young people, we are incredibly well-placed to try and improve.

As well as NDD, modern research in this field suggests that we should be promoting connection (and often reconnection) with nature. The term 'nature connection' is often used to describe the human–nature relationship through various lenses, from practical engagement to emotional affinity (Barrable and Booth, 2020). I explore this in some depth in my book *Bird Therapy* and there are many excellent papers and books on this subject, many of which can be found in the reference list. One of the overarching observations of most modern research into this is that we cannot simply provide opportunities to be outside and in natural environments; we have to offer clarity and structure on how we will facilitate the specific opportunities for nature connections. For example, one study suggests that nature connection activities should encourage emotional expression and tap into young people's affective domain (Chavaly and Naachimuthu, 2002). They offer specific ideas: arts-based programming, sensory awareness activities, and play; approaches I have tried to weave into *Inside/Outside* for this reason.

This outlook was backed up by OFSTED, albeit in an older 2008 report into learning outside the classroom, which it found was most successful when it was an 'integral element of long-term curriculum planning and closely linked to classroom activities' (OFSTED, 2008). However, a later systematic review found that the outcomes in outdoor learning research tended to be 'soft' outcomes such as communication and confidence, but the links to other topics and curricular subjects were lacking across all the research they reviewed (Fiennes et al., 2015). Clearly, I advocate for those 'soft' outcomes, but I find it interesting that cross-curricular links were deemed to be sparse; therefore, I have tried to incorporate a number of these into *Inside/Outside*.

I will leave you with a wonderful quote from Stephen Pickering (2017), in a book on creative outdoor learning (also published with Routledge). It is a quote that I feel is integral to this book:

> Teaching creatively outdoors involves teaching creatively indoors, too.

How to use this book

Inside/Outside is divided into three key themes, which are then broken down into key topics containing the five core strands of emotional literacy discussed earlier. The three thematic areas are:

- Emotions and feelings
- Self and situation
- Mental health and wellbeing

This book is designed to be used in several ways. The busy teacher can dip into it for general ideas and inspiration, but, equally, it can be used in a more systematic way. For each topic covered, you will find a series of class-based activities (the 'inside' of the title) that encourage reflection and introspection, and are placed over a double-page spread. These are then paired with an outdoor activity that mirrors the topic, for example, we may explore sounds and their potential therapeutic properties, by discussing sounds we like and know can calm us; we then go outside to experience, and map sounds for ourselves. Inside activities have a blue header strip on the pages and outside activities have a green one, as shown:

INSIDE

OUTSIDE

Introduction

The inside activities have been produced with a view to being able to slot into the KS3/4 PSHE curriculum, therefore, you will find that the class-based activities follow a similar and proven structure throughout. As well as for use in mainstream secondary schools, these activities can also be used in specialist, alternative, and health and social care settings as a programme for personal development. If you choose to deliver schematically, you do not necessarily have to do both the inside and outside activities as they are *designed* to stand alone or work in conjunction accordingly. I advise familiarising yourself with the activities and reading through them thoroughly before deciding how to deliver them, as you will know what works best for the young people you work with.

I would like to be clear that this book is also not designed to be prescriptive. As professionals who work with young people, we are all individuals, and such is the beauty of books like this to provide us with bones to add our own flesh to when it comes to delivery. One of the teachers at my old school initially struggled to embrace my emotional literacy programme and said this, which encapsulates how to approach this book:

> As an art teacher, I was struck by fear at the prospect of running emotional literacy lessons with my challenging form group. As a result, I would put off looking at the lesson plans until the day of the lesson. Having run the lessons exactly as they appeared in the scheme of work (sow), I realised that it need not be so prescriptive, and I now include art skills within the scheme.

With all of this in mind, *Inside/Outside* is suitable for anyone who works with young people, including but by no means limited to:

- SEND teachers who deliver a range of topics across different ages
- PD and PSHE teachers
- One-to-one workers
- Youth workers
- School leaders
- Home educators
- Anyone with an interest in the wellbeing benefits of nature.

Introduction

While it is aimed at young people in Key Stages 3 and 4, many of the ideas and activities in *Inside/Outside* can also be differentiated to be suitable for Key Stages 1 and 2.

Ideally, the exercises and activities in this book work best with small groups of young people, however, it is not so much about the number of young people you deliver them to, more the environment that you deliver it in. A shared 'community' approach to discussion – I can share – you can share – I can be vulnerable – you can be vulnerable – is how I approach every session, to help the safety net fall around the group. It also helps to promote empathy for others, which we know is one of the core strands of emotional literacy. I suppose that emotional literacy can be viewed narrowly, as a standalone but essential element of a school curriculum, and as a wider pedagogical approach to teaching. It is often described as a way of being and not of doing; with importance placed on creating the best learning environment for this to happen in. In all the research I have read, there is a clear emphasis on this and on the fact that any teaching around mental health should be 'delivered in careful sequences'. Therefore you will notice several repeated terms, approaches, and short activities throughout this book:

- Word starter – I generally use 'Hangman' but some may question the political correctness of this, so I have called it a 'word starter' throughout. I have seen a useful one where young people make as many words as they can out of the 'root' word, which often works well.

- Discussion – This and questioning are the skeleton of any work regarding wellbeing and reflection, and, if used effectively, can be the key to unlocking the group and the session.

- Mind-mapping – Tried and tested, simple and engaging. You cannot go wrong with these for collating thoughts and notes.

- Alphabet – Simply writing an A–Z on the board or on paper and getting your group to fill it with words that are connected to the topic. Tried and tested, simple and engaging. Ideal for hooking and expanding.

- General stationery – You will see this listed in the 'you will need' section and this refers to writing implements such as pens and pencils.

- Slideshow – You will see this listed in the 'you will need' sections and this means that you will need the downloadable slideshow and a way to display it to your group.

Introduction

If you plan to deliver any form of programme using these sessions and ideas, then I would recommend planning a short introductory session, perhaps as an activity within a session, or the length of a form time or assembly, to introduce it to the young people you will be working with. Here are some ideas of the kind of thing I have covered when doing this myself:

- Explain the duration of the 'programme' you will be running and why it is important – there are plenty of points in this introduction that you can impart.
- Facilitate a word starter using the words 'emotional literacy'.
- Ask the group members what they think it means, note down ideas, and formulate an agreed group definition.
- Hold a brief discussion on the sorts of theme and topic that the young people you work with think may be covered when discussing emotional literacy.
- Introduce a brief overview of the themes you will be covering. The three sections of the book are coherent here. I pre-plan how and when I'm going to drop the outdoor sessions in, too, and write up an overview/scheme/timetable that I also share with the group.

Section 1
Feelings and emotions

It is widely reported that the summative years of secondary education are some of the most stressful of our lives, with the pressures of examinations and the impending transition to post-16 settings adding additional stressors to an already challenging period – adolescence. The brain goes through a raft of changes in the teenage years. Research shows that almost all areas of the brain continue to develop through adolescence, particularly the prefrontal cortex and limbic system. These are the areas of the brain that are involved in expressing emotions, making decisions, and reading situations (Arain et al., 2013). With so much going on for them, even without the impacts of the pandemic, is it any wonder that the prevalence of mental ill health in young people is so high?

The DfE and its regulatory body, OFSTED, both outline the responsibilities of schools and education professionals in relation to mental health, which are also applicable to anyone who works with young people. However, this transcends so much deeper than what is taught in classrooms. In *Mental Health and Behaviour in Schools*, as well as the curriculum, we are told we must reinforce any teaching about mental wellbeing through school activities and ethos. Focusing on a culture that ensures the mental wellbeing of young people is supported across any setting is the gold standard, but inevitably, finances, curriculum constraints, and bureaucratic ties can stop this from happening. There are ways that you can weave teaching about feelings and emotions into other subjects and ways that you can let young people know that you are emotionally available. Try asking a random young person how they feel today as they are passing you in a corridor, surprise them, take the time to show an interest.

Do not change your identity as a professional working with young people, but please do reflect on how emotionally available you make yourself. Do you use your emotions in your work, to engage and connect with young people, or is your only focus on meeting arbitrary frameworks and standards? Outcomes are not just grades; equipping young people with the life skills they need to flourish in society is equally as important, but we cannot expect reciprocal emotional literacy if we do not demonstrate and model it ourselves.

Feelings and emotions

INSIDE

What are feelings?

- Identify and recognise a range of feelings, how they interlink and how we respond to them.

I have always found that teenagers struggle with the explicit labelling of feelings other than 'happy', 'sad', and 'angry.' In this session, we begin to explore two of the key strands of emotional literacy: self-awareness, and self-regulation. The feelings alphabet activity is an excellent way to extract more complex ideas from your group, although I find this requires regular prompts and charades from me to show emotions such as shock and fear. I have been able to stretch this activity over an entire 50-minute lesson before, by exploring all contributions in-depth. The feelings triangle then offers a solid visual for your group to begin thinking about how feelings arise; and you can find a wealth of online videos about the chemicals in the brain that cause us to experience emotion, if you wish to explore this further. It is important that when you conduct the group discussion at the end, you lead by example and share something yourself, to encourage the group to also share. I would think of this beforehand and have it noted down or to mind, so you are prepared to model this discussion to your group.

You will need:

- Whiteboard and marker
- Feelings triangle sheet
- Exercise books
- General stationery

1 Word starter

Use the word 'feelings' to facilitate a word starter of your choice.

2 Feelings A–Z

Facilitate a group discussion whereby you extract a minimum of one emotion/feeling for each letter of the alphabet; you may find that the group wants to produce more examples for each if they enjoy the activity (we did three for each). This activity can last a while if you are confident at utilising explorative questioning and discussion about some of the contributions. The group are to annotate into their books as you go.

3 The feelings triangle

Introduce the group to the feelings triangle on page 103 and discuss how the three sides of the triangle are interlinked. This can be done as a 'guess the three areas' activity, with a triangle outline drawn onto the whiteboard, or projected as a visual reference.

4 Group discussion

Ask your group and any support staff to think of a time when they experienced an intense feeling/emotion and then apply it to the triangle model – what was the thought, what was the emotion, and how did they respond? Share these in a safe-space discussion and discuss alternate ways that we could respond in that situation. The group to note the triangle into their books.

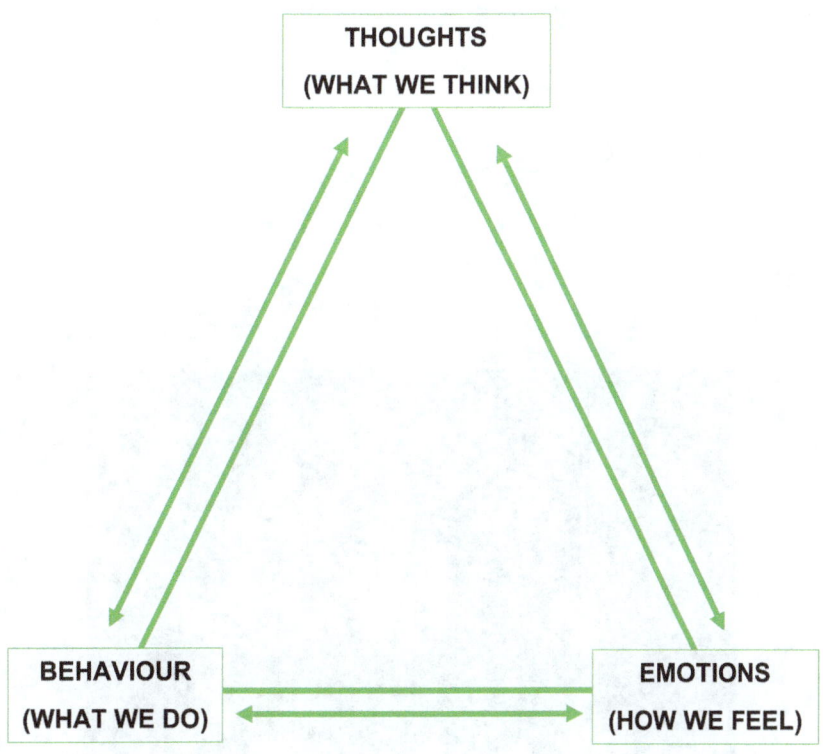

Feelings and emotions

OUTSIDE

Sonic sit-spot

- A simple outdoor activity that can be repeatedly adapted depending on the season, the setting, and the group.

There is an abundance of new research into the benefits of exposure and immersion in natural sounds. A recent study by King's College, London (Bakolis et al., 2018), found that there was a tangible improvement to wellbeing after contact with birdsong, trees, and even just from seeing the sky. As well as birdsong, other natural sounds have been explored, such as the sound of naturally running water. However, all studies have drawn the same conclusion: that natural sounds improve our wellbeing, both in the immediacy and up to several hours' after experiencing them. This activity was designed for my original teaching pack and proved to be popular across all age ranges, which is why it was a certainty to be included in this book. I have even seen this delivered effectively with a challenging group of all-male SEMH students who enjoyed showing me their completed sonar maps after the session.

You will need:

- Access to any outdoor space
- Your ears
- Sonar map sheet

1 Head outside

Find a spot with minimal background noise. This activity is best conducted in what would be deemed a 'natural environment', such as a woodland or field, however, it can be easily delivered anywhere there are a few trees or hedgerows. It is best facilitated April–June.

2 Ground yourself

Sit in silence individually and just listen to the birds. Allow yourself to really sense and feel the ground below you and the air around you; this is called grounding and we can also call this your 'sit-spot.'

3 Listen

When you are ready, close your eyes and listen to the sounds around you. Try to appreciate each individual sound as a passing moment. This is called mindful listening. Open your eyes and make notes on what you can hear. Which sound is the closest and which is the most distant? Use the sonar map sheet on page 104 to map all the sounds you hear according to their proximity.

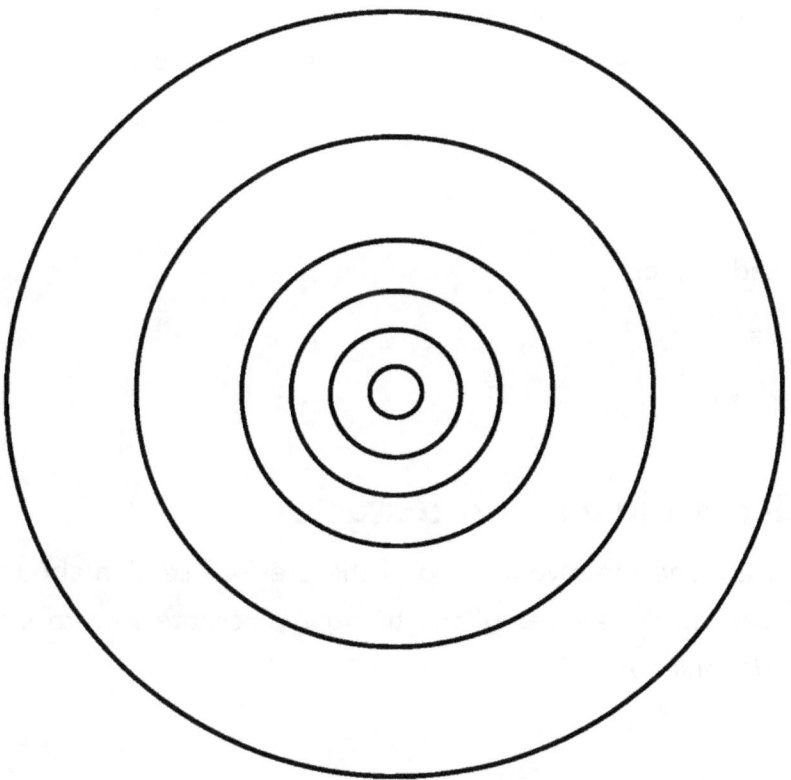

INSIDE

Regulating emotions

- Identify a range of our own triggers. Recognise the escalation curve and begin to consider our own responses.

This session follows on naturally from the previous one and continues to explore the same two strands of emotional literacy. It starts with a recap question to begin embedding key points and, as we know, this cycle and repetition should help to facilitate recall. The trigger activity can be triggering so ensure you know any difficult backgrounds in your group well enough to pre-empt any potential impacts. That said, I have run this with a small group of young people who all have trauma and attachment difficulties, and they were incredibly insightful and responsive. As with other adult-led activities, I shared my own triggers at the start to help create that safe bubble for the group to want to share in themselves. The escalation curve is a great visual to get your group thinking about their own behaviour. I have used this with several challenging young people, who have quickly recognised the reflection in their own dysregulated behaviour and have then been more open to discussing it. The final activity does need to be monitored as the group will often try to write the bare minimum, therefore, I float and check, and have also increased the number of examples, or asked for a paragraph rather than a sentence, depending on their ability.

You will need:

- Whiteboard and marker
- Exercise books
- General stationery

1 Recap discussion and word starter

Ask the group if anyone can give a recap of the previous session about feelings – can anyone remember the three areas of the triangle? Facilitate a word starter using the words *emotional regulation*.

Feelings and emotions

2 Mind-mapping activity

What are your triggers? Name three things that trigger an emotional response for you. These can be done on sticky notes or shared verbally, depending on the group. Record on the whiteboard as you go. Discuss how we all have different triggers and how the triangle from the previous session applies.

3 The escalation curve

Introduce the concept of the escalation curve. Draw the line and the numbers shown on page 105 onto the whiteboard and add the first point – calm. Encourage the group to try to name the remaining six elements of the curve using a range of questioning and clues to tease the answers from them. The group are to then draw a rough version of the curve in their books, or you can print page 105 and annotate.

4 How could you respond?

Get your group to copy the table below into their books. I have added the most basic of examples, which I then write onto the whiteboard and encourage the group to share their own examples to go in a 'group responses table' – or at the very least, I add one of my own. Your group are to then continue independently, adding a minimum of three examples of situations and positive and negative responses to it.

Situation	+ response	− response
Argument with a friend	Compromise	Fight

OUTSIDE

Counting birds

- Identify and count the birds you see in your school grounds within a set time limit.

This is another activity from my original teaching pack with the counting sheet provided by the excellent Field Studies Council, which makes a plethora of accessible laminated outdoor identification guides. Although simple, if coordinated effectively, this can make for a lovely relaxed outdoor session, and I've added in some extra maths activities in Section 3 to extend it indoors if necessary. Watching birds is proved to be beneficial for our wellbeing (Exeter University has done some excellent research in this area) and counting them is a natural and methodical extension of this. Over the page are four beautiful garden bird photos shared by my good friend Alan Dixon, who is an exceptional wildlife photographer.

You will need:

- Access to an outdoor space
- School ground birds sheet
- General stationery

1 Head outside
2 Count

Use the school ground birds sheet on page 106 and set a time limit to spot as many of the birds as possible, I would suggest 15–20 minutes. You could also record the number of each species seen and any extra species you encounter.

3 Crunch the numbers

Discuss the findings as a group. What was the most common bird? Did any birds favour a particular habitat? If you recorded the number of each species of bird, this can easily be developed into a simple maths activity – producing bar graphs or pie charts, for example.

Feelings and emotions

4 Extend

You can also extend this further by signing your school up for the RSPB Big Schools' Birdwatch, which takes place every January. It can be interesting to undertake this activity once in each season and then compare the results.

Feelings and emotions

INSIDE

Self-care and coping

- Develop our awareness of the different ways that different people cope with things and if those methods are positive or negative.

Conduct a cursory internet search of the term 'self-care' and you will find yourself in a crowded marketplace of wellbeing products. Teenagers are not as susceptible to (or interested in) scented candles and body scrubs, in fact every discussion I have had with them about self-care tends to throw up the same responses: smoking weed, sleeping, gaming, and punching walls. Some do have positive hobbies but are often too embarrassed to share them in front of their peers. I find it can be helpful for you and/or your support staff to share your own approaches to self-care; I love to share that I watch birds and trap moths – you cannot get geekier! The final activity is fluid, with the aim of creating a wall display or posterboard. I have facilitated this session with many groups and always find that the personal nature of this task gives them a strong sense of ownership over the finished product as well as a positive piece of completed visual work.

You will need:

- Whiteboard and marker
- Exercise books
- Art/craft/display materials
- General stationery

1 Recap discussion and word starter

Ask the group if anyone can give a recap of the previous session about regulating emotions. In this session, we will be looking at how we can try to manage these situations. Facilitate a word starter using the words *coping strategies*.

2 How do you cope?

Instruct your group to copy this table into their books and add at least three ways in which they cope then put a tick or 'yes' in whether it is positive or negative. Reconvene

Feelings and emotions

and collate all the group members' methods for coping into a table on the whiteboard, which they will annotate into their books as they go.

How do you cope?	Positive?	Negative?

Positive ways of coping tend to be aligned with our interests and things that make us feel good. This can also be called *self-care* and is something that we should try to incorporate into our lives where possible. This can be referred to as a *self-care routine* and for some people this may be something like having a bath in the evening to unwind, whereas for others it may be participating in an extreme sport!

Get your group members to create a poster using a range of images that depict the ways in which they personally cope. In a smaller group, you can always increase the poster size. I was lucky to have a teaching assistant who was an incredible artist and who helped me to create the wall display shown below. You could use our display as inspiration for your own using each individual poster around a central focal point such as this.

OUTSIDE

Design-a-duck

- In my book *Bird Therapy*, I write about lots of different types of duck. Ducks are awesome – why not design your own!

Along with the growing body of research into the wellbeing benefits of connecting with nature, there have been several studies into the specific wellbeing benefits of being close to bodies of water when we are outside. The Wildfowl and Wetland Trust (WWT) is currently facilitating a social prescribing project around this called the Blue Prescribing Project (WWT, n.d.), and has been involved in a plethora of research into this area. Water means waterbirds and when we talk about waterbirds, the most common and most easily recognised species are ducks! In my original teaching pack, I asked the supremely talented nature illustrator Jo Brown if she could draw me a duck outline for people to decorate as part of an activity – which she did. It made sense to transfer that activity into this book and so here you have a carbon copy of it. On page 107, you will find a selection of lovely duck photos courtesy of Alan Dixon. Now ... Get ready to design-a-duck!

You will need:

- Duck outline sheet
- Access to an outdoor space

1 Head outside!

This activity is a bit of fun.

2 Duck it up

Gather up loads of natural materials, such as twigs, leaves, grass, conkers, acorns etc. and then you can use the duck outline sheet on page 107 simply as guidance for an outline, or you can print it off on A3 paper to use as an actual outline. Either way, use the natural materials to design and decorate your own duck. This can also be facilitated as an indoor activity with arts and crafts materials, instead.

Feelings and emotions

Feelings and emotions

INSIDE

What do we need?

- Explore Maslow's hierarchy of needs and how it relates to different aspects of our lives.

Have you ever worked in a room that's just too hot, or doesn't have any airflow? Perhaps you have been doing a presentation and really needed to go to the toilet, or maybe didn't have time to fill up your water bottle beforehand? These simple needs can really affect our performance, so it comes as no surprise that if the young people we are working with do not have their basic needs met, they are not going to engage with us. If you are reading this, it is likely that you are a professional who works with young people, and I would expect that at some point you will have seen Maslow's hierarchy of needs. However, most young people have not and, when you place such a logical visual in front of them and explain that you cannot progress up the pyramid without meeting the needs of the level below, it regularly seems to be a proverbial lightbulb moment. I find that this then often triggers some meaningful discussions around their own needs as a foundation for the next tasks, reflecting on what the tiers of the pyramid are and mean and how they relate to a learning environment.

You will need:

- Slideshow
- Internet access
- Whiteboard and marker
- Maslow's hierarchy of needs sheet
- Maslow in school sheet
- Sticky notes
- Exercise books

Before the session, familiarise yourself with the five stages of Maslow's hierarchy.

Feelings and emotions

1 Starter discussion

Pose the question 'what do we need?', and clarify to your group that you mean 'what do we need to live a fulfilling life and to function?' Show the group slide 1, which depicts Maslow's hierarchy. There is also a sheet version on page 108 if required. Verbally outline the five stages, and then discuss/question if the group understands what each stage means. Explain/expand if necessary.

2 Guided activity

Get your group to draw a three-column table in their books. The left column will be the five stages of the hierarchy (get the group to write one at a time as they work to ensure there is space). The middle column is 'what is it?' where the group will give examples of what meets this need, for example, sleeping as a physiological need. The final column (right) is 'what could happen if this need is not met?' – which explains itself.

3 Independent activity

Hand out the Maslow in school sheet on page 109 and ask the group to independently work through and map how their needs are met at school – such as through specific lessons/subjects, by specific staff, or through accessing services. Reconvene and discuss as a group, reviewing any similarities and recurring themes.

4 Group discussion activity

Display slide 1 again and then give each group member a sticky note and ask them to write their name on it. Ask them to come up and stick their note on the pyramid where they think they currently are on the hierarchy. Discuss why they have placed themselves where they have.

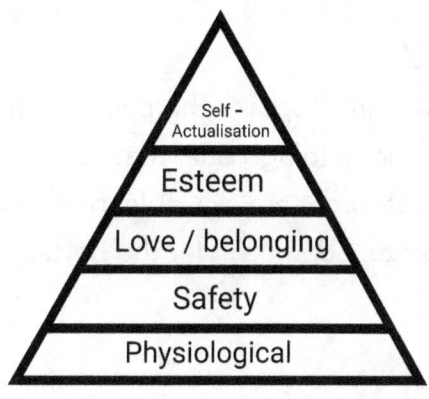

Maslow's Hierarchy of Needs

OUTSIDE

Natural colours

- An outdoor activity, like a treasure hunt finding various colours in nature. There are many colours in nature, and we often overlook this without truly taking them in.

A technique you will encounter often in nature writing is the vivid description of colours found in the natural world. As someone who has read a lot of nature writing but also spent a lot of time outside looking at natural things, I can categorically say that it does not matter how many superlatives someone uses to describe colour, nothing beats going outside and gorging your eyes on the wonder of nature; especially across the seasons, as there can be such a dramatic change in the palettes on display. This was also an activity in my original teaching pack, and it is a simple idea, inspired by a visit to a well-known DIY chain to choose some paint. Standing in front of a wall of colour (and ridiculous names), I found myself matching them to natural things – wildflowers, moths, and butterflies – through sheer boredom. We settled on a light bluey-grey in the end and I walked away inspired to turn the experience into an accessible activity. A successful shop visit all round!

You will need:

- Access to an outdoor space
- Paint swatches sheet
- Photographic equipment (camera, smartphone – if available)

1 Head outside!
2 Get colour hunting

Individually, in pairs or in small groups, take the paint swatches sheet on page 110 and find either a natural object or something visual that matches each colour. These can be noted down, collected, or, if resources are available, photographed. The aim is to find all the colours in one outdoor place. So, the wilder the better.

Feelings and emotions

3 Extend

You could take the objects back inside and use them as a discussion starter, such as, who found the same items? Or, were there any that you couldn't find? You could also use the found items to create a display, a nature table, or a piece of creative art.

Feelings and emotions

INSIDE

Fear and phobias

- Identify what a phobia is, share and discuss our own fears.

I decided to put this topic in as I felt it encompassed all five strands of emotional literacy; and fears are a subject that often arises in other discussions in these sessions. To recognise our own fears is part of self-awareness and as fear causes an emotional response, it can also be part of our self-regulation. We can show empathy towards the fears of others and perhaps help them deal with those; thus, strengthening relationships. Finally, a fear can be motivating (think extreme sports) and debilitating, so naturally feeds into our own motivations. This was added to the original programme later, after it came up in a session and I planned these activities to tackle the topic. I did source lots of pictures from the internet to represent the fears and made a basic slideshow, which you may want to add to the base presentation yourself as it did work well. Do think about your own fears prior to the session and consider discussing them with your group. I found that my groups tended to remain quiet on their own fears for Activity 2 until I shared my own, which, incidentally, is the sea. Use your own fear as a catalyst for your group to share theirs.

You will need:

- Slideshow
- Whiteboard and marker
- Internet access
- Top ten fears sheet
- Exercise books
- Sticky notes

1 Recap discussion and word starter

Ask the group if anyone can give a recap of the previous session about Maslow's hierarchy of needs. Can anyone remember the five stages? Facilitate a word starter using the word *phobia*.

2 Introductory discussion and sticky notes activity

Ask your group what they think a phobia is. Discuss and define. Look at the definition on slide 2 and get them to copy the first paragraph into their books. On a sticky note, get each group member to write down the thing they are most scared of. Collect these and keep until the end of the session.

3 Whole-group activity/quiz

Write the numbers 1–10 in books and time five minutes for your group to try and guess the top ten fears in the UK. Come together and share the top ten fears sheet on page 111, which are the actual top ten. Can anyone guess what these ten weird words mean? If not, research them together as a group and annotate the sheets to define each one. You can also discuss any others that people have guessed, as this will generate further discussion.

4 Group discussion and independent task

What are the ingredients for a genuinely scary story or film? Can you think of any? This is always a good time to chat and share any stories. Invariably, someone will have a 'ghost' story to share. Guide your group to complete the questions about their own fears, found at the base of the top ten fears sheet.

5 Final group exercise

Retrieve the sticky notes from Activity 2 and share them with the group. Try to guess whose fear is which – it's harder than you think! The key point here is that it's tough to predict people's fears as they are unique and internal to the individual.

Feelings and emotions

OUTSIDE

Counting insects

- Identify and count the common insects you can find in your school grounds within a set time limit.

Although numbers have been shown to be in decline, insects are still everywhere we go to. As I personally took more of an interest in the wildlife around me, it became impossible for me not to notice insects in a general sense. Their variation is incredible: colours, markings, behaviours, camouflage, habitats, eating habits – the list goes on and on. There is just so much to like about them and take an interest in if you want to. The majority of the places that you might visit to specifically connect with nature should theoretically be buzzing with insect life, especially those that are managed for biodiversity. I was first enamoured by hoverflies and Green Hairstreak butterflies, residing in a gorse-filled glade in the first summer I started taking an interest in birdwatching. Do not underestimate the awesomeness of insects. This activity follows the same format as the bird and wildflower activities earlier in the book, with yet another fantastic spotting sheet provided by the Field Studies Council.

You will need:

- Access to an outdoor space
- School ground minibeasts sheet
- General stationery

1 Head outside
2 Count

Use the school ground mini beasts sheet on page 112 and set a time limit to spot as many of the insects on the sheet as possible, I would suggest 15–20 minutes. You could also record the amount of each species seen and any extra ones you encounter.

3 Crunch the numbers

Discuss the findings as a group. What was the most common insect? Did any insects favour a particular habitat? If you recorded the amount of each species of insect, this can easily be developed into a simple maths activity – producing bar graphs or pie charts, for example.

INSIDE

Anger

- Reflect on what anger is and how different people experience it.

In every setting I have worked in, I have supported young people who identify as having problems with managing their anger; or who clearly do have issues with it and require additional support and approaches. We begin to teach children how to manage and express their anger from a very early age, often starting when we ask a toddler to express it in a way other than physical. In teaching older children to recognise anger and what can cause it, we are taking the first steps in helping them to develop an alternate outlook to it and how they can respond. This session encourages them to reflect on when they were last angry and then widens this into a group activity. There are also several worksheets adding visual elements to the session. I particularly like the final activity, where I have had some lively discussions with young people about what they think constitute healthy and unhealthy ways of managing anger. We also see deeper spiralling of learning topics here, with connections to sessions on feelings and coping strategies.

You will need:

- Slideshow
- Exercise books
- Signs of anger sheet
- Anger cycle sheet

1 Starter question and discussion

Pose the question 'what is anger?' to your group. Facilitate a brief discussion around what individually and collectively they feel it is. Ask if anyone is willing to share the last time they felt angry and what caused them to feel that way. It can be powerful for you or a member of your support staff to do this, helping to create a safe space for sharing in.

2 Longer activity

Write an alphabet onto your board and encourage your group to contribute to an 'anger alphabet', made up of words they feel are, or could be, associated with anger. I ask for three words for each letter and this always produces lively and competitive discussion. Encourage your group to copy into their books as you work through the alphabet together.

3 Individual reflective activity

Hand out the signs of anger sheet on page 113. Your group must match up all the signs of anger that they recognise in themselves from the grid and either circle, or highlight, whichever they prefer. Afterwards, get your group to stick these sheets into their books.

4 The anger cycle

Hand out the anger cycle diagram sheet on page 114. Discuss how this is like the feelings triangle (another good opportunity to spiralise learning). Ask your group the following question: is anger a primary emotion or a secondary one (i.e., always caused by a primary one)? This makes for some insightful points. Studies show that it is always a secondary emotion, with another emotion underlying it.

5 Managing anger

We have discussed coping strategies in an earlier session – do we manage our anger in the same way? Ask the group how they manage their own anger? And create a mind-map of anger management strategies. Discuss whether they are healthy and/or unhealthy and label with a 'h' or 'u' accordingly; this can be done in two different coloured pens.

OUTSIDE

Sensory sit-spot

- A simple outdoor activity which can be repeatedly adapted depending on the season, the setting, and the group.

I originally used this in a lesson on World War Two bombings, encouraging my group to reflect on the sensory experience of being caught up in such a horrific event. A much more serene approach to this sensory task is to apply it to a natural environment. It works well in tandem with the natural colours activity and was originally an extension of that activity in my earlier teaching pack; but it stands alone well, and I have used it with several different groups to good effect and observed others facilitating it effectively, too. Depending on the level of need in your own group, you may have to take a considerable lead and identify some of the sensory experiences yourself or prompt your group with clues and questioning. I have also included four senses so that they can be removed to accommodate any sensory impairments you may also have in your group profiles. You could also supplement this with the later texture bingo activity.

You will need:

- Access to an outdoor space
- Sensory sit-spot sheet
- General stationery

1 Head outside!

As per the mindfulness bird sounds activity, head outside and find a safe and secluded spot that you can sit in. This activity is best conducted in what would be deemed a 'natural environment', such as a woodland or field; however, it can be easily delivered anywhere there are a few trees or hedgerows.

2 Get sensory!

This session will consider four senses: sound, smell, sight, and touch/feelings.

3 Embrace!

In your sit-spot, shut your eyes for a few minutes and embrace the sensory surroundings that you are in. On the sensory sheet, note down the things you can hear, smell, and feel. You can then open your eyes and consider what you can see, noting it all down on the sensory sit-spot sheet on page 115.

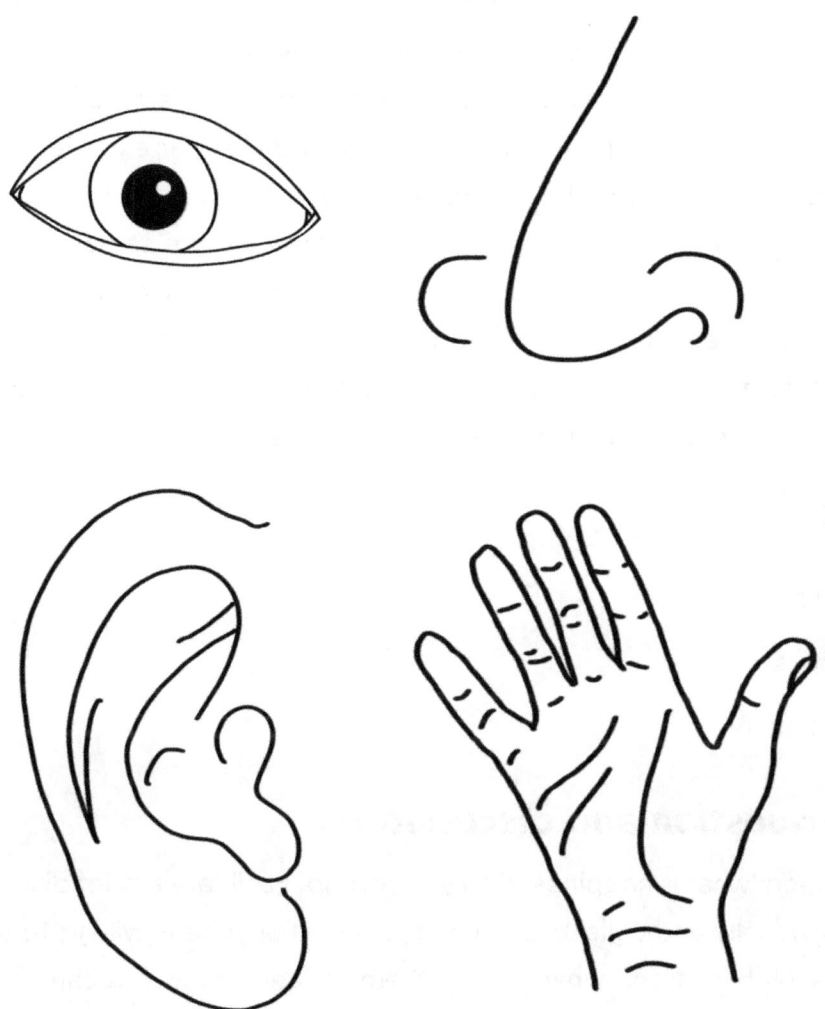

Feelings and emotions

INSIDE

Happiness

- Reflect on what happiness means to us and what we think makes us happy.

With any emotional literacy intervention or session, there is often a tendency to lean towards deficit models and negative themes, therefore, it is not only nice, but also incredibly important for us to cover the positive aspects of wellbeing in any work that we do. As part of developing our self-awareness, it is essential that we can recognise and acknowledge the things that make us feel good, as well as bad. As adults, it is easier for us to do this based on our wider lens on the world and our experiences, but I have found that it can be much tougher for young people. In fact, I have found that some of the things they identify as bringing them happiness are the same as their identified coping strategies in our earlier session. As well as the activities in this session, there are also several short videos available online that explain the chemicals in our brains that are responsible for feelings associated with happiness. I find that the science behind the emotion, in video format can help embed the concepts of this session further.

You will need:

- Whiteboard and marker
- Exercise books
- General stationery

1 Starter question and discussion

Pose the question 'what is happiness?' to your group. Facilitate a brief discussion around what they individually and collectively feel it is. Ask if anyone is willing to share the last time that they felt happy and what caused them to feel that way. It can be powerful for you or a member of support staff to do this, creating a safe space for sharing in. Write the shared examples onto the whiteboard and reflect and discuss with your group what they think happiness is. Try and tease out a definition from them, which will ultimately be unique to your group, but ensure that you reinforce the key point that happiness is different for every one of us.

2 What makes us happy?

Pose the question – what makes us happy? It is highly likely that someone will call out 'money' or 'sex' – ask them both how and why? It is also likely that they will not have an answer to these! Start a mind-map and in the middle of it, write 'what do WE do that makes us happy?' Complete the mind-map with your group, discussing the things that they do that makes them feel happy. Here is a facilitator list of some more reflective things that you can add and are proved to promote happiness:

Gratitude

Positivity

Good relationships

Giving/being kind

Meditation/yoga

Flow – losing yourself in something you love

Sport and exercise

Self-confidence

Contact with nature

3 Three things activity

In their books, get the group to write three things they are happy about today: 'Three things I am happy about today are …' Allow them a few minutes to complete these sentences. Come back together as a group and share them to see if there are any correlations. These things are things that we are grateful for and this introduces the idea of gratitude, which we will explore more deeply in the next session.

4 Plate of dreams

This final activity is a bit of fun. On a large sheet of paper (at least A3) either you or a group member draw a 'plate' (basically a flat oval) and then hand out three sticky notes to each group member. On your notes, write your absolutely favourite meal in the form of a starter, a main course, and a dessert. This is your 'plate of dreams'. Stick them all on the plate, discuss, have a laugh, and see if there are any correlations in meal choices!

Feelings and emotions

OUTSIDE

Gratitude scavenger hunt

- A simple outdoor activity that can be repeatedly adapted depending on the season, the setting, and the group.

Gratitude is another positive topic and, again, it is something that young people may not recognise or be able to express. However, gratitude has become a prominent feature of much mental health work, the premise being that if we regularly appraise the things that we feel grateful for, the more grounded we become; thus, improving our wellbeing. Most of the approaches to gratitude that are used in therapeutic interventions with young people and with adults use a written approach, generally referred to as a gratitude journal. These journals create a reference point to those things that we are grateful for, however, what it can also do is create a vortex into the past, of things that we *have* been grateful for and not ground us in the present moment. With this activity, I have tried to make those participating in it connect to their surroundings and use their senses to identify things around them that make them feel good. I had considered planning the theme of gratitude as a class-based session but opted against it in the end as I felt it would be better to explore and promote nature connection alongside. The simple checklist I have provided in the appendices offers some parameters and security, but it is an individualised task, asking young people to think about natural objects in a different way than they may have previously done. This activity also works well in conjunction with the natural colours and texture bingo activities.

You will need:

- Access to any outdoor space
- Photographic equipment (camera, smartphone – if available)
- Gratitude scavenger hunt sheet

1 Head outside!
2 Concept

Explain that there are so many wonderful things to enjoy in the natural world, but we are often too busy with our phones and busy lives to appreciate them. This scavenger hunt is an opportunity to connect with the things we find ourselves personally drawn to in an outside space and celebrate them.

3 Get hunting

Agree a time limit for the scavenger hunt and hand out the gratitude scavenger hunt sheets on page 116. There are five extra blank columns so that you, or your group members, can add your own items to search for. The group can self-manage this activity to a degree if they are able to. The aim is to get all, or as many things as possible, marked off on the checklist. They can be noted down, collected, or if resources are available, photographed. Here are five sample items, the rest are in the appendices:

Find:

- a colourful flower
- something that makes you smile
- a leaf shaped like a random animal
- something that smells amazing
- your favourite tree

4 Extend

You could take the objects back inside and use them as a discussion starter, such as who found the same items? Were there any that you couldn't find? You could also use the found items to create a display, a nature table, or a piece of creative art.

Section 2

Self and situation

When considering the structure of this book, the first task was to work out how to fit all the strands of my emotional literacy scheme of learning into it. I originally tried to overlay the scheme with the five core strands of emotional literacy, but this got a bit messy and resulted in two sections of the book, feelings, and mental health; leaving a weird mix of themes that I could not pigeonhole in either section. I looked more objectively and noticed that many of the 'leftover' themes straddled the topics covering who we are and how/why we interact in certain situations. Thus, the third book section arose – self and situation.

The development of a sense of self is considered a key developmental task during adolescence (Pfeifer & Berkman, 2012) and the process results, often later in adulthood, in us creating our own secure narrative of our lives, defining who we are. This can be incredibly stressful and confusing for young people and can impact on mental health and overall wellbeing. The aim of this section of the book is to offer a basic framework of sessions that help the young people we work with to start becoming more self-aware. Self-awareness is indeed one of the five core strands of emotional literacy, and it is interesting that the adolescent brain, with its changes in the limbic and prefrontal areas, intrinsically struggles to recognise and empathise with others, let alone with self. This transcends to the situations, interactions, and relationships that young people navigate – particularly during adolescence. Simply put, if you are not in tune with yourself, then how can you tune in with other people?

The inside activities in this section of the book explore what makes up who we are, and the outside ones encourage us to reflect on where we sit and how we are part of the places around us, in both a geographical and an emotional sense. You could consider this as 'our situations' and as I mentioned in the first paragraph, the idea of situation also transcends into the inside activities in this section (neat, huh?). We explore the topics of conflict, communication, friendships, and respect; and as well as covering the strand of 'self-awareness', this section also delves into the strand of relationships and relates to the strand of empathy, too. As before, you can dip in and out or follow the framework as it is written; and everything you need is included in the appendices.

DOI: 10.4324/9781003331988-3

INSIDE

Self-awareness

- Define what it means to be self-aware and be able to identify at least three of your own attributes.

The concept of 'self' used to be considered a stable and singular representation of who we are. However, recent research suggests that as our 'selves' transcend multiple aspects, our 'self' is a transient and ever-changing thing, responding to the situation or context that we are in. There is a far more damaging and difficult context now, in the form of social media. We strive to share the perfect self-image with others and therefore, we often create a construct for others to see that is not representative of our actual self. Many young people behave like this, and I am not claiming that they all have multiple personalities; more that they create multiple representations of themselves and, ultimately, may feel lost a lot of the time. I designed this session to start off the theme of self and situations and get my group to consider what makes them who they are, which continues in the next inside session. The sticky notes activity can be a real eye opener and I was both shocked and pleased to see several young people choose various teachers they encountered through schooling, as two of my three selections were also teachers of mine. The final flower activity has quite a hefty explanation and I would recommend quickly having a go at drawing and annotating the flower prior to the actual session.

You will need:

- Whiteboard and marker
- Exercise books
- General stationery
- Sticky notes

1 Intro discussion and word starter

Introduce the fact that we are moving on to a new theme called 'self and situation'. Ask the group what sort of things they think we may be covering. Facilitate a word starter using the word *self-awareness*.

2 Discuss and define

Ask the group what they think it means to be self-aware? Discuss and agree on a definition and then note the group definition into books.

3 Sticky notes activity

All group members and staff write down on a sticky note the three people they feel have had the most impact on them as people, shaping who they are today. Encourage group members to reflect as they share and ask them to help classify the people into categories such as family, friends, celebrities, support services (teacher, youth worker etc.), and anymore that come up. In most groups, family and friends will top the list and this can be an interesting discussion point.

4 Group discussion + activity

On a whiteboard, draw a large flower with five petals and a round centre. Allow space around it, as each petal will have small images at its outer edge. These images are a clock; two stick people; an eye and an ear; a brain; and a smiley emoji. Write the words 'event/issue' in the centre of the flower and then lead a discussion, employing a range of questioning techniques to tease out the things that can influence how we respond to an event or issue. These are our five petal images and represent our: past, present, and future; experiences as a person; sensory experiences; thoughts; and feelings.

This is the 'flower of awareness' and I use the analogy of 'blooming' with it as a visual. After choosing an example of an event/issue – we used a fight with a close friend to work round the petals – discussing and filling all the things that could happen around an issue that we are aware of. I encouraged my group to copy and annotate the flower into their books.

Self and situation

OUTSIDE

Texture bingo

- Explore, identify, and record a range of textures in an outdoor environment.

Textures are all around us in the natural world. We mainly experience texture visually and can appreciate its aesthetics, but it is not often that we stop to touch something and take the time to appreciate how it feels, what temperature it is, or what it smells like. You see, when you stop to take a moment and appreciate the natural world a bit more (a key theme in all these outside activities), you start to notice more of the details and intricacies to be found in the things we often overlook. This activity, although simple, is highly effective and I have seen it delivered in a range of settings from specialist to Forest schools. I have tried to make it as simple as possible but have also included a wide range of textural adjectives to encourage exploration. These can be found collectively on a large bingo card in the appendices.

You will need:

- An outdoor space – this is best conducted in an unknown place, such as a woodland, but is equally as accessible in any size of outdoor school space
- Texture bingo sheets

1 Intro discussion and safety

Start at an agreed meeting point. Hand out the texture bingo sheets on page 117 and encourage your group to individually, or in pairs, try and find a natural item that matches the words on their texture bingo cards. For example, they may find a smooth leaf, such as Holly, or a rough piece of bark.

2 Timings and adaptations

You can set your group a clear time limit on this activity to fill as little or as much time as you wish. There are several ways you can 'score' the bingo cards:

- You could operate it on a trust basis and ask your group members to just mark them off as they find them.
- They could note down the location as well, so theoretically they could be checked.

- They could use camera phones to take a photo of the textured object (depending on your policies), and this could also feed into an ICT-based task whereby they are arranged in a word document or such like.
- You may have access to photographic equipment they can use.
- If it's viable to do so, they could collect the items so that it becomes more of a 'texture scavenger hunt'. These could also be used to make a nature sensory table or tray, back in the classroom.

Self and situation

INSIDE

Identity

- Identify a range of traits that make up our identities.

Adolescence is a time of change and exploration. One of the primary contemplations for young people is to start trying to find out who they are, where they sit in the social constructs that we have made for ourselves, and how they wish to be perceived externally. In working with young people, we view these things from that external perspective. We see trials in style, in interests, and in expression; conformity and rebellion often converging before our eyes. It is fascinating for us as professionals but can be deeply challenging for the young people we work with to navigate. Research has found that we can support this process through 'explorative learning experiences' and states the importance of any work on this theme taking place in a supportive learning environment, something we have already looked at in this book (Verhoeven et al., 2019). The main task in this session, the identity tree, was one of the first I did with my own emotional literacy class one year and they engaged with it brilliantly. To be honest, I thought the task might be a bit overcomplicated, but they really engaged with the roots and branches analogy.

You will need:

- Whiteboard marker
- Exercise books
- Identity tree sheet
- General stationery

1 Group activity – I am

Taking turns, group members, and staff to complete the sentence 'I am …' and describe themselves, for example 'I am funny.' This can generate some lively discussion. I usually record the adjectives in a mind-map, as they create a list of group attributes. The group could also note these down in their books.

2 Independent task – identity tree

Hand out a large piece of paper (we used A3) to each group member. They must rotate the sheet vertically and draw a *very basic* tree shape on it. They will need to draw a line across the page 1/3 of the way up from the bottom – this will be the ground – and below this must be some basic roots – above the ground there must be a trunk. This task is split into two parts.

Part 1

This involves the completion of the leaves of the tree and reflecting on various elements of our identities. Please see identity tree sheet part 1 on page 118.

Part 2

This involves answering some deeper questions about the things that have shaped and influenced our identities and then forms the roots of our trees. Please see identity tree sheet part 2 on page 118.

One of my group members used some mini-sticky notes to make their leaves, and there is nothing to stop this becoming a more creative and arts-based activity.

Self and situation

OUTSIDE

Sense of place – street work

- Explore the area around our setting and focus on the houses in our urban environment.

Much of the writing and research about connecting with your local area looks through a lens of nature and green spaces. Yes, both are beneficial for wellbeing, as are proximity to water and local biodiversity, but sometimes this is just not accessible or viable. I wanted to create an activity that took all the 'nature 'spotting' and 'collecting' approaches in this book and applied them to the streets around our focal point. Human geography. This activity aims to widen young people's sense of place, a concept defined as the 'symbolic relationship formed by people, giving culturally shared emotional/affective meanings to a particular space or piece of land' (Low, 1992). Place means more than just what we see, it is also what we think and feel, when immersed somewhere. Therefore, I believe it is important to motivate young people to recognise the urban locus around them in terms of place; attaching meaning to things they would usually pass off as mundane, such as the streets and houses explored in this activity.

You will need:

- Access to the local area close to your setting
- Recording implements, either paper and pens or a mini-whiteboard and pen

1 Intro discussion and safety

Start at an agreed meeting point, discuss, outline, and be clear about your own agreed safety rules. Dictate the list of items that your group must find. Ensure that they note them down so they can mark them off themselves – I usually tell them twice just to be sure. I find that mini-whiteboards work well with this activity, but pen and paper does as well. Divide your group up either individually or in pairs/small groups to go and find the items on the street bingo list, which are listed here:

- a golden letterbox
- a gravel driveway
- a house with a name, but not a number

- a white house
- a doorstep
- a doorbell
- a skylight
- a street name sign
- a triangular porch roof
- an outdoor light
- a garden gate
- a red-brick wall

2 Regulations and adaptations

You could set a clear time limit on this activity to fill as little or as much time as you wish. There are several ways to 'score' the bingo cards as per the texture activity:

- You could operate on a trust basis and ask your group members to just mark them off as they find them.
- They could note down the location as well, so it could theoretically be checked.
- I would advise against taking photographs of people's houses in the interests of safeguarding.
- You could assign each party to a specific street as this allows for comparisons such as, who found the most?
- Group members could keep a tally if they find more than one of a bingo item and this can be adapted further into a range of maths-based activities.

Self and situation

INSIDE

Conflict

- Demonstrate an awareness of how we can resolve and manage conflict situations.

Conflict can play a massive part in the lives of young people, and we know from several sources that young people with any type of additional need are more at risk of abuse and therefore of being involved in conflict situations in general (DfE, 2022; NSPCC, 2022). Conflict can transcend all spheres of a young person's life. It can spill out onto social media platforms, escalate incredibly quickly, and, ultimately, have a huge impact on overall wellbeing. I have found that there is a need to take care when discussing conflict with young people as it can generate some heated opinions and sharing of stories. You may also need to employ careful and empathetic management of your group and it is important to consider young people who may be experiencing or have experience of trauma before you begin exploring the theme of conflict.

You will need:

- Slideshow
- Exercise books

1 Word starter

Facilitate a word starter using the words *conflict resolution*.

2 Discuss and define

As a group, discuss the term 'conflict', come up with a definition together and get your group to write it into their books. Show them slide 3, which shares several definitions. Encourage and allow time for the group to expand their definition.

3 Group activity

Move onto the slide 4 – this asks group members to place the word 'conflict' in the centre of a mind-map, then, in one colour, write as many *types* of conflict they can think of and, in another colour, add as many *causes* of conflict as they can. This can be recorded on scrap paper or in books, individually or in groups, and then collated as a group mind-map on the whiteboard by you or a volunteer.

4 Group and independent activity

Here we are looking at the Thomas Kilmann model of managing conflict.

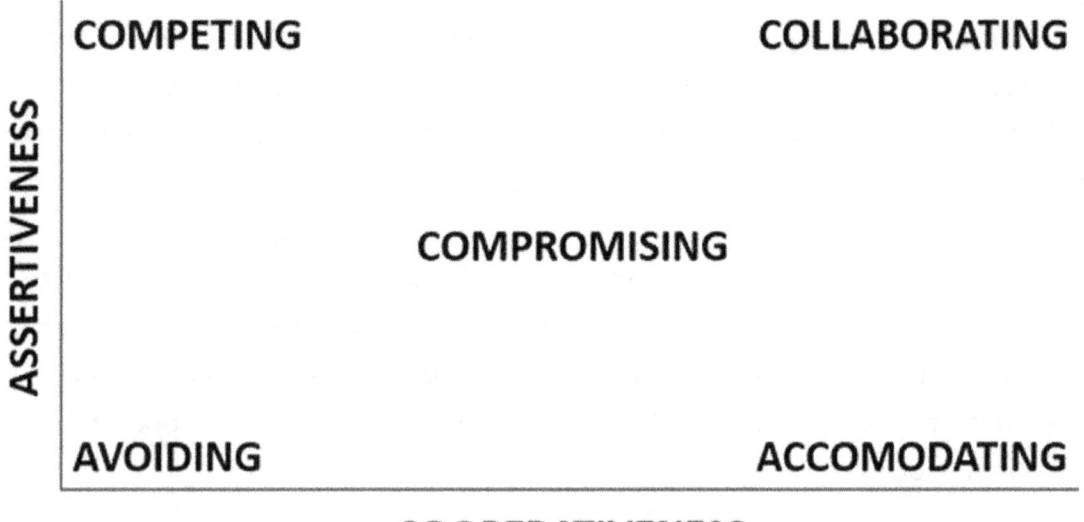

Talk through slide 5, which shows the Thomas Kilmann model of managing conflict. This is used by HR professionals around the world and shows 5 'styles' of managing conflict. If your group need individual visuals, you can print the slide off in advance of the session. Encourage group members to point out where they feel they sit on the matrix – this could be recorded with sticky notes or marked on the whiteboard.

Slide 6 then asks the group to list as many different strategies for resolving conflicts as they can think of (using the Thomas Kilmann model for inspiration) and label each of them with a + if they think they are positive and a – if negative. Come together after an agreed time and discuss as a group … just don't argue about it.

OUTSIDE

Our habitats

- Consider the habitats in our nearby surroundings and how they interlink, culminating in the creation of artistic, colour-based representations of it.

This activity, and many of the other outside activities in this book, can be related to a single line from a study of outdoor teaching by Scottish Natural Heritage (Mannion et al., 2011) 'All pupils valued opportunities to get to know a natural place beter.' Key, here, is that concept of 'place' – how somewhere appears visually, what its purpose is and how it evolves over time. These three areas are part of the significance that we, as humans, attach to places, and, within this book, I have tried to approach place both obviously and covertly from a range of angles. For example, in this activity, we explore it in terms of our senses, but also how they make us feel. This simple but structured activity asks us to seek out the places where we and other creatures may reside, and then map them using colour and creativity. Afterwards, there are many things that you can do with your squares, including, for example, making a giant interconnected patchwork representing habitats in the local area.

You will need:

- Access to an outdoor space
- Our habitats sheet
- Selection of colouring implements

1 Head outside

We are specifically looking for places where a range of different landscape features converge. If you can do this away from the school site, at a nature-dedicated site, then … amazing! But really, I'm talking about where a hedgerow meets the school field, or a few trees overhang. Obviously, the more biodiverse the environment, the more reflective this activity becomes, but it doesn't require a visit to a nature reserve or anything.

Self and situation

2 Find your sit-spot

As per some previous outside activities in this book, find yourself a sit-spot. When you feel grounded, use your senses to investigate and explore the habitats around you. Imagine being a bird – where would you perch? Imagine being a mouse – where would you hide from predators? Imagine being a slug – where could you hide during the day? As you consider these (and other similar questions you can pose to your group), begin to consider the different habitats and homes for wildlife that sit in your nearby space.

3 Map the habitats

Use the key and the layout below to create a colour 'map' of the four spots in the four squares. This grid can be found in the appendices as a template on page 119, named 'our habitats'.

Self and situation

INSIDE

Communication

- Explore why we communicate, some barriers to communication, and consider the importance of visuals when we communicate.

As professionals, how often do we hear or say ourselves that 'the communication wasn't good enough'? If you conduct an internet search of the most common workplace problems, communication is always on the list. On reflection, imagine being in a position where you are trying to work out who you are, individually and socially, and then having to communicate your needs and wishes on top of that? It cannot be easy at all. Communication is a vital component of emotional literacy, and it underpins all the key strands in some way, especially relationships. However, to communicate effectively, you must first create the safe, secure, and nurturing environment required for delivering any of these sessions and activities. In this session, you will encourage reflection on a range of areas concerning communication, including the reasons why we do so and some possible barriers to it being effective, the aim being to recognise the importance of communication in a general sense.

You will need:

- Slideshow
- Whiteboard and marker
- Mini-whiteboard
- Exercise books

1 Word starter

Facilitate a word starter using the word *communication*.

2 Group discussion and mini-whiteboards (if available)

Why do we communicate? Ask each group member to write three reasons why they think we communicate on their mini-whiteboard. Then collate the answers one at a time and write onto the whiteboard. You can tally as you go and see what the most selected reasons are. I tend to take a photo of this and then print it, but if you are unable to do that, your group members can note it in their books.

3 Group discussion and activity

Move onto slide 7, which shows images representing four barriers to communication. They are *what we can do, where we are, how we feel, and who we are*. Group members to divide a page in their book into four and, first, try to guess what the four images may represent. As a group, discuss and add examples to each section, noting them down as you discuss and work through them. The four sections can also be titled disability, environment, emotions, and identity/culture, if the other four suggestions are too abstract for your group.

4 Group activity (pairs) – non-verbal communication

Pair the group members up and sit them facing one another, with one facing the whiteboard and one with their back to it. Project a reasonably complicated image of your choice (I use an old man in a suit playing a full drum kit) and the group member facing the board must describe what is in the picture to their partner (who has their back to it), using only non-verbal cues and body language. The group member with their back to the whiteboard will have a pen and paper and must try to draw what the other is describing. *No sounds/words are to be used.* This can be a hilarious and difficult activity. Set a time limit (5 minutes is good) and then pull the group back together afterwards to discuss. Use some leading questions about how it felt to not be able to speak and have a look at how the pictures came out.

5 Closing discussion and visual

Explain to the group that there are three 'Vs' of communication in a model created by researcher Albert Mehrabian (Mind Tools Content Team, 2022) and ask them to guess what they are (visual, verbal, and vocal). Visual is body language, verbal is what we say, and vocal is how we say it. Ask group members to guess what percentage each of them makes up of a complete pie chart. Show slide 8 (the actual figures) and get your group to note this in their books. Reflect on the importance of visuals such as body language, when communicating.

OUTSIDE

Mindfulness in nature – birdsong

- A simple outdoor activity that can be repeatedly adapted depending on the season, the setting, and the group.

Birdsong is a wonderful thing. From the dawn chorus itself, to its role as a beacon of hope for British soldiers in the World War Two trenches, it has long been associated with restorative properties. A 2013 study found that birdsong was the sound that participants most associated with their own restorative experiences with nature (Ratcliffe, 2013). It has even been played through a children's hospital radio to help calm patients. This exercise encourages your group members to ground themselves and then consider the bird sounds around them. By calling them bird sounds, we expand from birdsong to consider the other calls they make. These are usually contact calls between individuals or groups as they feed. They can also be warning sounds, known as alarm calls, signalling the presence of a nearby predator to all the birds in the vicinity. It may be that your participants do not even recognise what sounds are made by birds. This can generate some interesting discussions and debates as to what some natural sounds are and in the case of birds, it could be worth showing your group the website XenoCanto, which is essentially a catalogue of bird sounds; and you could also cross-reference the common bird species in the earlier counting birds activity with it.

You will need:

- Access to an outdoor space
- Your ears
- Possibly the sonar map sheet
- Possibly some note paper and writing equipment

1 Head outside

Find a spot with minimal background noise. This activity is best conducted in what would be deemed a 'natural environment', such as a woodland or field; however, it can be easily delivered anywhere there are a few trees or hedgerows. It is best facilitated April–June.

Self and situation

2 Focus on the bird sounds

Sit in silence and just listen to the bird sounds around you. Allow yourself to really sense and feel the ground below you and the air around you; this is called *grounding*. Focus on the silence between the bird sounds as well as the sounds themselves. This is your sit-spot.

3 Next steps

You can talk your group through the next steps, or you could have them printed/handwritten as prompts to help them. Make a mental note of:

- The bird that is nearest to you and what it sounds like.
- The bird that is furthest away and what it sounds like.
- Can you hear any groups of birds?
- Can you hear a conversation between birds and, if so, what do you think they are saying to one another?
- Are the birds concentrated in one area or habitat?
- You could at this point, use the sonar map sheet (page 104) to map the bird sounds, too.
- Regroup and discuss all the above points.

Self and situation

INSIDE

SWOT analysis

- Recognise what a SWOT analysis is and identify our strengths, weaknesses, opportunities, and threats.

As is always the way with something business related, the SWOT analysis template is attributed to one person and then contested by several others. However, it is clear is that it originated in the corporate world as a tool for strategic planning and development. I came across this during my teacher training as a way of analysing my own performance. More recently, I realised that it could be a great exercise to do with the young people I work with, especially when I started to put together my emotional literacy programme. This is always an interesting session, with the group often needing some prompts to identify their strengths; although they usually seem much more able to recognise threats and weaknesses. The way that this session flips from being reflective for the individual to then being for the whole group is perfect for embedding the key emotional literacy strands of empathy and self-awareness. The natural progression from self to the group to an external body makes for a well-structured and ever-evolving session.

You will need:

- Whiteboard and marker
- Exercise books
- General stationery

1 WOT is a SWOT?

Write the letters S-W-O-T on the board. Explain to your group that this is a model for analysing yourself and your performance. Try to tease the four words (strengths, weaknesses, opportunities, threats) from the group using questioning and clues. Before you move on, get your group members to split an exercise book page into four and label each quadrant with one of the four elements of a SWOT analysis.

2 Discussion

Facilitate a deeper reflective discussion where all group members reflect and contribute to a whole-group SWOT analysis. I have had just half of this activity take up the rest of the session before and had to carry it over to the next one.

3 Group statement

Use the group SWOT to generate ideas of how the identified areas (predominantly strength, weakness, and threat) affect learning as a whole group. Write a short paragraph that describes the group (seriously) considering the SWOT – for example – we are opinionated, savvy, and loud.

4 Business SWOT

SWOTs are also used in business to analyse a company status. Your task is to choose a brand/shop/organisation that you like and conduct a mini-SWOT on it. Some ideas for your group could be a sportswear brand such as Nike or Adidas or a tech brand, Samsung or Apple, for example. Follow the same four-square quadrant model as used in Task 1. If a group member completes one SWOT, then suggest a different area, such as fast food, and encourage them to complete another. Below is an example of a completed SWOT from one of my own group members. It is interesting that they were able to reflect on the present, with their strengths and weaknesses, but not on the future, with their opportunities and threats.

Strengths	Weaknesses
Art	Ego
Calm under pressure	Competitiveness
Photography	Worrying about what people think
Music	Being a sheep
Want to improve (creativity)	Forgiving people
Opportunities	**Threats**
Going to college	Negativity
Going to studio	Lack of support

OUTSIDE

Signs of sustainability

- A bingo-style activity, investigating your local area for signs of sustainable and eco-friendly living and then mapping them.

You may already be familiar with the terms 'climate' or 'eco' anxiety and what they mean. If not, they generally refer to our affective responses to the negative impacts of climate change. This is still a new area of research but is becoming increasingly prevalent in young people and can lead to significant depressive and anxious symptoms. Research suggests that professionals who work with young people must first try and instil pro-environmental behaviours before trying to teach about the science of climate change and how to take direct action. With that in mind, this activity encourages young people to explore and investigate their local area (planned or in the immediate vicinity of your school or working space). While out, they must find ten different signs of sustainability or things that people have done, or are doing, that help the environment. I appreciate that you may not be able to do this easily, depending on your location, so you could adapt it and conduct a survey of your school or working space and then suggest adaptations. This could also be conducted as an inside activity, using an online map platform to explore a chosen area.

You will need:

- Access to an outdoor space
- Writing equipment
- Signs of sustainability sheet

1 Intro discussion and safety

Prior to heading out, agree safety parameters as per any localised geography walks. Assign specific streets/areas to groups/pairs or choose somewhere away from the locality that you have researched beforehand. Hand out the signs of sustainability example sheet on page 120 and encourage the group to individually, or in pairs/small groups, go and find the items listed next, some of which are shown on the example sheet (these are the ones highlighted in **bold** in the list):

COMPOSTER	**BIRD TABLE**	**SOLAR PANEL**
FRUIT TREE	**BIRD FEEDER**	**GREENHOUSE**
WATER BUTT	**GARDEN POND**	**WIND TURBINE**
GLASS MILK BOTTLES	**INSECT HOTEL**	**DOUBLE GLAZING**
FOOD WASTE BIN	**WILDFLOWERS**	**VEG PATCH**
HEDGEHOG HOUSE	**GARDEN WASTE BIN**	**ELECTRIC CAR**
FRUIT TREE	**RECYCLING BIN**	**WEEDS**

2 Recording and extensions

The idea of this activity is that the smaller groups are competing to find the most sustainable street or area. They must loosely map their area on a separate sheet of paper, marking roughly where each 'area of sustainability' is. As with all my observation/collection-type activities, this is designed to promote deeper noticing and appreciation of things that usually pass us by daily.

There are several follow-up activities that you can do, starting with facilitating a reflective discussion on the findings:

- You could discuss basic comparisons, such as who found the most and were there any areas with a high concentration of people living more sustainable lives?
- Group members could keep a tally if they find more than one of a bingo item and this can be adapted further into a maths-based activity, such as producing bar graphs or pie charts.
- If you plan the activity to take place exclusively on local streets, you could use the rough sketches to make a sustainability map display.

Self and situation

INSIDE

Respect

- Identify and define what respect means, generally, and for us as individuals.

While reading up on teaching the concept of respect to teenagers, there was an observation that came up many times – why do we often speak to and treat young people in a way that we would not want to be ourselves? I leave the question mark there as I want you to think about it. The example I read about reflected on the way we speak to younger children, but still applies – 'what's the magic word?' – and, as what I was reading stated, you would not say that to your friend would you? Respect, in many ways, is innate, and I struggled at times to think of how to create a session that instilled it for the young people I work with. But really, we should be modelling respect daily, and it should be a two-way process whereby we earn the trust of another through being considerate and empathetic, then they mirror it back. Therefore, this is a collaborative session that encourages inquiry and reflection on the constructs that young people find themselves in, often encouraging some insightful reflections.

You will need:

- Whiteboard and marker
- Exercise books
- Person outline sheet
- Realising respect sheet

1 Word starter

Facilitate a word starter using the word *respect*.

2 Agree on a definition

As a group, discuss the meaning of the term respect. Ensure you steer your group to recognise that respect can vary for every individual. Collaborate to decide on a collective definition and write this into books.

3 Group activity

Group members to have two of the person outline sheets on page 121, one for what a respectful person looks like and one for a disrespectful person. I suggest that you draw the outlines on the board and complete as a group activity, with group members annotating their own sheets. However, they could also do this independently depending on their overall group profile.

4 Independent activity

Group members are to draw the two tables below in their books and complete independently. This is not an activity to share, just for self-reflection. Encourage them to think of five people for each table, from all aspects of their lives, including famous people.

Who I respect	Why?
Who I do not respect	Why?

5 Independent sensory-based activity

Use the realising respect sheet on page 122, which is essentially just the sensory sit-spot sheet from section 1, with the 'smell' section removed. Encourage the group to complete the sheet, thinking about what respect looks like, feels like, and sounds like. Examples could be that it looks like eye contact when talking, feels like a safety net, and sounds like kind words.

OUTSIDE

Counting wildflowers

- Identify and count the common wildflowers and plants that you see in your school grounds within a set time limit.

This is a variation of the bird-counting activity from my original teaching pack with the accompanying sheet again provided by the Field Studies Council. Wildflowers are a vital but declining part of the English countryside. They are important in many ways, as a food source for pollinators, a habitat for various animals, and as an aesthetic wellbeing enhancer for humans. As well as being rooted in our ecosystem, they often share their roots with folklore and medicine, too, and when their flowers die off, their seeds provide a food source for birds and other wildlife. They are brilliant in their versatility. In principle, most of us would look at a school playing field (for example) and think that it was devoid of flora, but, if you examine more closely, you will see that there are wildflowers along the edges and in the cracks. These marginal growths are often overlooked as weeds, but, in their flowering seasons, even the spindliest plant can bloom with beautiful flowers. Although simple, if coordinated effectively, this can make for a lovely relaxed outdoor session in the summer months, and as per the counting birds activity, I've added in some extra maths activities in the third section to extend it indoors if necessary.

You will need:

- Access to an outdoor space
- School ground plants sheet
- Writing equipment

1 Head outside
2 Count

Use the school ground plants sheet on page 123 and set a time limit to spot as many of them as possible, I would suggest 15–20 minutes. You could also record the number of each species seen and any extra species you encounter.

3 Crunch the numbers

Discuss the findings as a group. What was the most common plant? Did any plants favour a particular area? If you recorded the number of each type, then this can easily be developed into a simple maths activity – producing bar graphs or pie charts, for example.

The following pictures were provided by my good friend, natural history writer, Jon Dunn. Clockwise from top left: Primrose, Creeping Thistle, Selfheal, and Ragged Robin.

Self and situation

INSIDE

Friendships

- Reflect on what friendships are and when they can be unhealthy.

This session was written in response to some peer issues we were experiencing at my last school. While those issues were specific to that setting, I observed at the time that many of the young people I have worked with often perceived a peer as a 'friend' when it was apparent from outside that it was perhaps not a healthy or reciprocal relationship. I wanted to encourage them to reflect on what constitutes being a friend and how healthy friendships function. What I found was that they were clearly able to identify the attributes of a positive friendship and very quick to realise that they struggled with these; and, on deeper reflection, many would also state that they did not feel they had any 'real' friends. Obviously, this requires sensitivity and care to support this, and, in my own sessions I was open about my own minimalistic approach to friendships. You may want to consider how you approach this yourself in preparation of any session.

You will need:

- Slideshow
- Whiteboard and marker
- Exercise books

1 Group discussion

Do you consider yourself as a good friend? How many good friends do you have? How do you define friendship? As a group, agree a definition of what friendship is and write into books.

2 Mind-map activity

What makes a good/healthy friend? Complete a mind-map of all the attributes that you, as a group, think makes up a good/healthy friend.

3 Discussion with visual

Look at slide 9 with the image of a set of scales on. Discuss what could unbalance a friendship. This is solely here as a discussion point and can be drawn out or short, depending on engagement. I have used sticky notes to annotate this diagram directly on the board or have written around it if young people are engaged.

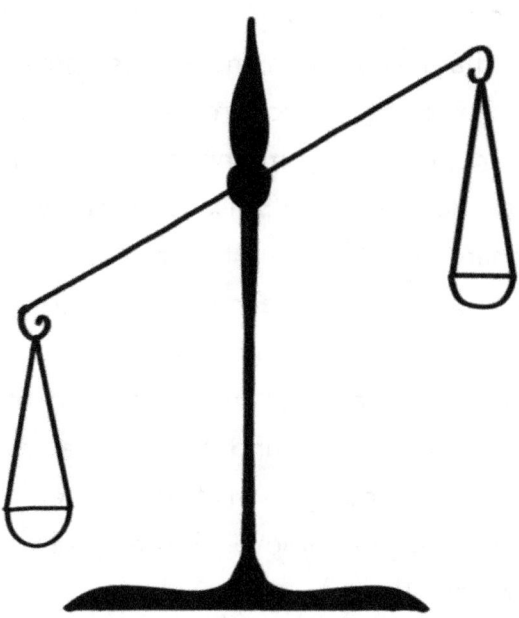

4 Group activity

Slide 10 contains four friendship scenarios. Group members are to draw a two-column table in their books, one with a tick and one with a cross. For each scenario, they are to write a positive and a negative response to it, into their table. This can be done as a group or individually.

5 Final discussion questions

Have you ever had to end a friendship? How did you do it? Why did you feel that it had to end?

Self and situation

OUTSIDE

Bling up a butterfly

- As I became more interested in wildlife, I discovered that butterflies are awesome! Just like the duck in Section 1, it's time to bling up your own!

As I became more interested in birds, naturally I became more interested in wildlife, generally. The next genus that I took a genuine interest in was lepidoptera, specifically, butterflies. A lot of the places that I started birdwatching in were also fantastic habitats for butterflies, and, the more I noticed them, the more I began to recognise and identify the more common species. Butterflies are brilliant creatures. Even the plainer ones are beautiful and graceful. There are also many that are *incredibly* aesthetically pleasing, too. People like butterflies. They often attach personal and spiritual meaning to them. They are vital components of ecosystems around the world, as pollinators themselves and as indicators of the ecological health of an area, as it is noted that wherever there is an abundance of butterflies, there is an abundance of other invertebrate life. As per the earlier duck activity, in the appendices, you will find a butterfly template for this activity and overleaf, you will find a selection of lovely butterfly photos for inspiration. Now… Get ready to bling up a butterfly!

You will need:

- Butterfly outline sheet
- Access to an outdoor space

1 Head outside

This activity is a bit of fun.

2 Bling it up!

Gather up loads of natural materials such as twigs, leaves, grass, conkers, acorns etc., and then you can use the butterfly outline sheet on page 124 simply for guidance on an outline, or you could print it off on A3 paper to use as an actual outline; either way, use the natural materials to design and decorate your own butterfly. This can also be facilitated as an indoor activity with arts and crafts materials, too – it works well both ways.

The following four images were provided by my friend, naturalist, and wildlife photographer, Alan Dixon. Clockwise from top left: Painted Lady, Peacock, Common Blue, and Meadow Brown.

Section 3

Mental health and wellbeing

Just before completing this book, the NHS released the third and final wave of research in its series of surveys on the mental health of children and young people (NHS Digital, 2022). There are some scary statistics in the summary, most tellingly that, in 2022, 18% of children aged 7 to 16 years had a probable mental health disorder. That is almost one in five, or six, in the average classroom. A further 10.8% young people on top of that have a possible mental health disorder as well, which makes it almost 30% of young people of school age who potentially require mental health support in the UK.

If you conduct an internet search to try to find out about mental health support in UK schools, a rosy picture is painted of easily accessible services available to all young people. Unfortunately, for those of us who work in frontline roles, we know that this is not the case. Waiting lists are immensely long, referral processes can be difficult and drawn out, and, very often, young people do not meet the threshold for support and therefore end up with nothing in place. For those who do end up receiving support, the gulf in quality across counties and commissioning areas means that there can be huge disparities in the interventions and treatments received.

Therefore, as discussed in the introduction to this book, our role in educating, supporting, and sometimes just listening to young people should *never* be underestimated. This book section has been designed to help you to do all three. There are activities that will generate discussions about mental health that you and young people may not have had before. There are activities that will encourage deep reflection into what it is like to live with poor mental health. There are activities that will offer alternate perspectives and challenge misconceptions. These are the inside ones, however, and this chapter really comes alive when it heads outside. A sensory poetry activity and some outdoor meditations are buffered by a variety of hands-on creative activities; taking tough topics from your group space and heading outside to use the mind and body to connect with nature.

Mental health and wellbeing

INSIDE

What is mental health?

- An explorative introductory session to start conversations about mental health and what it is.

When discussing mental health, an expression I hear often is that it is 'something we all have', it just varies as to whether it is good or bad. This is such a simple but effective way to explain the term to young people, in the way that it is the same as us all having physical health, but again, this can vary from person to person and be affected by the choices we make. I tend to hammer this fact home to the groups I work with. The Mental Health Foundation also use a strong analogy, comparing our mental health to the weather (Mental Health Foundation, 2022), as it is completely changeable and fluctuates through the year, with seasonal changes and dramatic dips and troughs. This session uses some of my dependable activities – starting with a definition, moving on to a group alphabet, and then to an independent activity, before pulling it all back together at the end. These activities have also been designed to encourage deeper reflections on mental health and, by this stage, if you have created that safe space for your group to express themselves in, then you should be leading an insightful discussion, particularly during the alphabet activity.

You will need:

- Slideshow
- Exercise books
- Whiteboard and marker
- Person outline sheet
- Sonar map sheet

1 What is mental health?

Introduce the fact that we are moving on to a new theme called 'mental health and wellbeing'. As per the last change of theme, ask the group what sort of things they think we may be covering. Ask your group what they think mental health is? Discuss and agree on a definition. Look at the definition on slide 11 and copy into books. This is largely considered to be the best definition of mental health. Ask the group, if they are willing, to raise their hand if they have been affected by mental health, or if someone they know has. You can then ask if anyone with their hand up is willing to elaborate, but also, only do this if you are comfortable doing this yourself.

2 *Mental health alphabet*

The classic alphabet activity works well with mental health. Write an alphabet onto your board and encourage your group to contribute words associated with mental health conditions, physical responses, emotional responses, and sources of help. If you have been loosely following the sessions, by this point, there should be lots of causal links, such as depression, alcoholism, risk taking. As mentioned earlier in the book, I ask for three words for each letter and this always produces lively and competitive discussion. Encourage your group to copy into their books as you work through.

3 *Good and bad mental health*

Utilise the person outline sheet on page 121 again and give two copies of it to each group member. Get them to label one as 'good mental health' and one as 'bad mental health'. Set a time limit and ask them to independently complete an outline with a representation of what they think both good and bad mental health look like. For any young people who are not as comfortable with arts-based activities, you can offer the opportunity to label and annotate their people with words that reflect this.

4 *Circles of support*

Discuss with your group that we all have circles of support around us. These circles radiate outwards in the same way as the sonar map, therefore, you can use the sonar map as the worksheet for this activity, too (page 104). Your group members are to label the small central circle 'me' and in the first circle write the names of the people who they feel they are closest to and who provide them with the most support. As the circles move away from the centre, they must continue labelling the circles with other people who support them until they get to the periphery, where they may place community members, group leaders, and so on. You do not have to discuss these individually, but, obviously, you could compare them as a group.

OUTSIDE

Have-a-go-at-haiku

- Haiku is an accessible approach to poetry. Take your group outside, immerse them in their surroundings and have a go at writing some.

Haiku is a short form of imagery-laden poetry that originated in Japan. Each haiku adheres to the following set of conventions. They always feature elements found in the natural world. They always contain 17 syllables, split over three lines in the ratio of five-seven-five. They always feature a seasonal reference, called a *kigo* in traditional Japanese haiku. They are always written in the present tense, and they do not rhyme. In the middle of the haiku, usually at the end of the second line is a 'cutting word' called a *kireji*. At this point, there should be a natural pause and a subject change – a 'twist' if you like. For such a small number of words, they require a great deal of patience and discipline to write, which is why I believe it is perfect to get outside, practise some outdoor mindfulness, and put some haiku together.

You will need:

- Access to an outdoor space
- General stationery

1 Head outside

This activity is designed to be facilitated outside but, if necessary, you could also go out and take photos if the weather is not so good and then take them inside to use as inspiration for writing your haiku.

2 Ground yourself

Encourage your group members to sit near you, but in a place that they like or feel comfortable in. Encourage them to really sense and feel the ground below them and practise their grounding, as we have done in other outside activities in this book.

3 Prep the group

Once grounded, read aloud the haiku rules in the opening paragraph of this activity, encouraging your group to note down the key points as you read. Using the writing equipment, you have given them, whether that is paper, their books, or whiteboards, the group members must produce a haiku, based on the spot they have chosen.

4 Get more specific

Allow the group members some autonomy to explore, encouraging them to find a natural object, such as a tree or an insect, observe it, then produce another haiku based on what they observe.

Below is one of my own nature haikus for inspiration, this one is about the Silver-studded Blue butterfly, a heathland specimen, which is abundant on several heaths local to my own home.

Flecked with tangerine. Icecaps melt on frosted steel. Summer's silver spark.

Mental health and wellbeing

INSIDE

Poor mental health

- A late addition to the book, this activity delves further into mental health, specifically looking at what constitutes poor mental health.

This was not one of the original sessions in the programme, but as I neared completion, I realised that it was a vital but missing component of the final book. Way back in the introduction, in the section titled 'why emotional literacy?', I noted that one of the statutory requirements of health education is to inform young people about how to recognise the early signs of mental wellbeing concerns. In a world that, post-pandemic, has seen a near 25% increase in general mental health concerns just across the adult population (World Health Organization, 2022) the benefits to our younger generation of being able to recognise and act on early warning signs is of utmost importance. This session uses a range of approaches, from scoring one's own mental health, to placing ourselves on a visual continuum, before using scenarios to decide when and how we would act if we recognised the signs and symptoms of poor mental health in someone we knew.

You will need:

- Whiteboard and marker
- Sticky notes
- Mental health scenarios sheet

1 *How do you feel today?*

Ask your group members to score their mental health today from zero to five, with zero being poor and five being amazing. Hand out a sticky note to each group member and ask them to write their initials and score on it and keep it to one side.

2 Mental health as a continuum

Display slide 12 to the group, which shows mental health as a continuum model. Explain that a continuum is a set of things on a scale that have gradual differences between them, and that, in this example, mental health and mental illness can be the parameters of a continuum. The diagram on the slide shows a visual representation of how the two areas interact. Discuss with your group about how we can sit anywhere on this scale between mental health and mental illness. Encourage your group members to come up to the board and stick their sticky note from activity 1 on to the continuum where they feel they presently are.

3 Signs and symptoms

First, facilitate a brief discussion on what signs and symptoms of poor mental health are. In this activity, we will consider *signs* as indicators in ourselves and in others, and *symptoms* as things that we or others experience. The three-column table below (with examples in) is also on slide 13 and, if you can project it into a whiteboard, it makes a handy template to write directly on to. Work with your group to list/name as many signs and symptoms of poor mental health as you can think of, into the three categories.

Physical	Mental	Social
• Stopped shaving and washing as well as usual	• Feeling more anxious	• Not responding to messages

4 Mental health scenarios

On page 125, you will find five mental health scenarios. The preference for this activity is that you facilitate your group to deliver a series of roleplays of each scenario and then suggest and discuss what they would do to support their friend. However, if your group are not confident with a roleplaying scenario, then it can be facilitated as a written task, too.

Mental health and wellbeing

OUTSIDE

The A–Z of noticing nature

- A combination of my go-to inside task with elements of several of my outside ones makes a simple, but effective observation and collection activity.

This activity takes some of the most effective elements of this book and combines them into one collective activity. It is inspired by my friend Vicky, who designs and runs wellbeing programmes for a regional wildlife trust. It takes that classic indoor alphabet activity outside, underpins it with elements of the five ways to wellbeing and encourages a mindful and sensory-based approach to nature connection throughout. The structure of the alphabet is such an uncomplicated way to add parameters to a task and people of any age just love to find and collect things, especially when they are pitted against one another in some way. This activity is all about honing our noticing skills, but it almost acts as a summative assessment of all the things that have been covered in this book. It also tests you as a facilitator, as you are very likely to be asked what certain things are, so that group members/groups can fill up their alphabets. I would suggest a 'recce' of your chosen location and to also have a look at some natural items for the more difficult letters of the alphabet in advance.

You will need:

- Access to an outdoor space
- General stationery
- Existing sheets noted in Section 1
- Additional equipment noted in Section 2

1 Preparation

Consider the location that you will use to facilitate this activity. It is best undertaken somewhere with a reasonable amount of biodiversity to enhance the productivity of the overall activity. It can also help if your group have completed some of the other outside activities in this book and can have the results to hand, specifically our habitats and sonic sit-spot. It can also be useful to have the three spotting sheets (birds, insects, and wildflowers) as they can help to steer your group towards finding, or at least observing, natural items for their A–Zs.

2 Tool up

I would suggest using a three-way approach to this activity, making it a mix of observing, collecting, and recording. Depending on the size of your group, get them to work independently or in pairs:

- *Observe* using all their senses alongside learning from these sessions, to notice and/or find something natural for each of the letters of the alphabet.

- *Record* in either their books, paper (clipboards are useful), or, if you are super prepared, then laminated paper or whiteboards, with markers. They can also record using photographic equipment if available, or even through sketching.

- *Collect* natural items for the alphabet using a receptacle such as a tub or tray.

How you choose to bring your group together and collate/share the results is entirely up to you, but the activity is more about the experiential learning experience than completing an alphabet (just save telling your group that until after!).

INSIDE

Depression

- Openly discuss depression, develop our knowledge of how it affects people, and consider other factors that can impact it.

The consensus across various sources is that depression is the most prevalent mental health condition on the planet; however, it is difficult to find any reliable data about the number of people with it. Depression is still incredibly misunderstood and along with all other mental health conditions, carries huge amounts of stigma for those afflicted. Everyone occasionally feels down, but when it lasts for prolonged periods of time, impacting you in myriad ways and sucking all enjoyment out of life, then not only is it a problem but it needs to be treated, too. I have heard many young people trivialising depression, mocking others through a lack of understanding, or claiming to be 'depressed' when I have a secure enough overview of them to know that they are not. The key to tackling this and the wider stigma around depression is to educate our young people; and while this is only a brief session on depression, embedding this kind of basic knowledge is vital.

You will need:

- Slideshow
- Internet access
- Mental health quiz sheet
- Whiteboard and marker
- Exercise books
- Depression word search

1 Intro discussion and word starter

Specify that today will be focusing on depression and that it can be a difficult subject. Try to pre-empt who may be emotionally affected and plan strategies accordingly. Ask for a show of hands for anyone who has experienced depression – either themselves or through someone they know. Facilitate a word starter using the word *depression*.

2 Video

At this point, I suggest showing your group a video called *I Had a Black Dog, His Name Was Depression*, which can be found on YouTube and is 4 minutes 18 seconds long. This animated short, depicts depression in the form of a dog, following the protagonist. I tend to show it, wait a few seconds, then calmly ask the group what they thought. I advise watching it prior to the session, so that you can comment, too.

3 The depression triangle

Share slide 14, with the unlabelled red triangle on. There are three elements of our health that go on the sides of the triangle, use a range of questioning techniques to tease ideas out of your group – the three areas will be revealed with a click on your electronic device. Ask the group to copy the triangle (you could also print the slide) and add annotations to the board of examples for each section. Some examples are shown below, but there are more that you can add:

- Physical – genetics, hormones, disability, weight, exercise, diet.
- Mental – anxiety, stress, mood, personality, self-esteem.
- Social – loneliness, isolation, friendships, relationships, work.

4 Quiz

Using information from the leading UK youth mental health charity Young Minds and NHS survey data, I have created a true or false quiz relating to young people and depression/mental health. This can be found on page 126, with the answers noted in red text under each question. It is likely that misconceptions will arise during the quiz, so discuss these with your group if they do come up.

5 Wordsearch

On page 127, you will also find a wordsearch of various words associated with depression.

OUTSIDE

Nest building

- Use natural materials to build a nest, thinking about a range of external impacts to shape the construction.

A nest is, literally, a space or shelter, used by or created, by an animal (usually a bird) to lay their eggs and then shelter their young in. Sometimes, when someone is struggling with depression, they may feel like curling up in a ball, staying in bed and shutting out the world – not too dissimilar from a bird stowing itself away on its nest until its eggs hatch. I first saw this activity when we took our daughter on a nature trail at a local National Trust property. She really engaged with it, and I could see then that it would benefit a range of young people to take part in this simple but meaningful outdoor activity. This is also the closest to what I would consider as a Forest school activity in this book.

You will need:

- An outdoor space that contains a range of natural materials, although twigs and branches are useful

You could also pre-collect materials if there are not any in proximity to where you are doing it.

1 Location and preparation

You can't just build a nest anywhere; first, you must consider the location from a range of perspectives. Ask your group to pick their own individual site for their nest, thinking about shelter, safety, access, materials, and food sources. They could also build their nest in, for example, a hollow in the ground or raise it off the ground entirely; it is up to them to get creative.

2 Get building

Guide your group to collect a range of sticks and twigs to form the basic structure of their nest. The nest must be built and there are lots of ways they can be assembled.

Mental health and wellbeing

They could weave the twigs to strengthen their nest, pile them up in a perpendicular pattern, or just hash it together and see what happens. I would suggest that they put some thought into this to ensure they make the most reliable nest they can.

3 Make it warm

Birds line their nests with lots of different materials to keep their young warm. Some example materials are downy feathers, moss, grass, animal fur, mud, straw, and leaves. Guide your group to collect softer wild materials to line their nests with once the outer structures are complete.

4 The nest factor

For a bit of fun, you could always judge the nests as a competition as to which one is the best and award a prize of some description to the winning one. Be sure to explain the rationale behind the winning one, such as the strongest core or the warmest lining.

INSIDE

Anxiety

- Identify what anxiety is, develop our knowledge of how it affects people and what other factors can impact it.

The NHS states that it is normal for young people to occasionally feel worried or anxious, especially during times of transition (NHS, 2019). However, if it begins to affect them daily, then it potentially needs to be countered with help and support. Anxiety can afflict us from birth and be exacerbated by adverse childhood experiences and traumatic life events. As discussed earlier in this book, adolescence is riddled with change and transition, thus, is a time of potentially huge amounts of stress for young people. It is natural for them to struggle with these feelings and events, but we are in a unique position to guide, support, and equip them with strategies as they navigate this difficult period. I have delivered this session to many young people, and it is a simple, but effective way of encouraging them to consider anxiety both generally and regarding themselves.

You will need:

- Whiteboard and marker
- Mini-whiteboards
- Markers
- Slideshow
- Exercise books
- Anxiety mind-map sheet
- General stationery

1 Intro discussion and word starter

First, ask a few recap questions. Perhaps ask what the topic in the last session was and what was on the three sides of the depression triangle? Then facilitate a word starter using the word *anxiety*. Pose the question 'what do we mean by anxiety?': 'A feeling of unease, worry or fear. We all feel anxious at times, but anxiety may be a mental health problem if your feelings are very strong or last a long time' (NHS Digital, 2022).

2 Mini-whiteboards of worry

Hand out mini-whiteboards and then encourage the group members each to write three things on them that they worry about. Get them to hold up their boards, share, and discuss. The key point to draw out of this discussion is that we all worry about the same and completely different things at the same time. If you want to record this, you can use slide 14 as a visual prompt to complete a mind-map of things that your group worries about, collectively and individually. A template for this can also be found on page 128 (anxiety mind-map sheet).

3 Symptoms of anxiety

The key question is what does anxiety look and feel like for different people? Project the table on slide 16 onto the whiteboard and then write onto the board, guiding the group to think about both psychological and physiological symptoms. Encourage the group to copy as you add their contributions.

4 Situation and response

If you think back to the session on regulating emotions in Section 1 of this book, we looked at situations and then how we respond to them positively and negatively. This activity is similar but encourages your group to consider things that they are aware of that have made them feel anxious (nervous, uncomfortable, worried, or edgy) and then how they responded to that situation. The group must copy and complete the table below independently, adding a minimum of three examples of anxiety situations and their responses to them.

Anxiety situation	My response
Going to a social event and not really knowing anyone	Basically, clung to my friend all night and followed them round

Mental health and wellbeing

OUTSIDE

Nature mandalas

- Create our own mandala patterns using natural items.

A mandala is a geometric pattern made up of concentric circles around a focal central point, a bit like the classic kid's stationery toy, the Spirograph! The word 'mandala' means 'circle' in the ancient language of Sanskrit and the iconography of the mandala has been around since the first century. The Swiss psychiatrist Carl Jung is credited with introducing the concept of the mandala as a therapeutic tool to the Western world, after he and his patients drew them in their sessions. He described the symbol of the mandala as a 'safe refuge of inner reconciliation and wholeness' (Klerk & Jung Society of Utah, 2015). The idea of making artistic mandalas is that we channel our attentions into the creation of the shapes and nothing external to these. This simple activity encourages us to make our own mandalas using natural resources – connecting to our self, as per Jung, but also to the materials that we can find outside.

You will need:

- Access to an outdoor space that contains natural materials; these could be collected beforehand if necessary

1 Clear a space and mark the hours on a clock

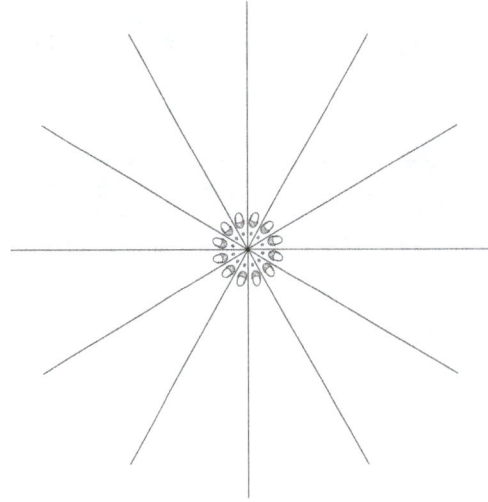

Mental health and wellbeing

2 Collect items from nature in multiples of 12

3 Start with small items in the centre; they could be seeds or nuts. Then add rounds to the clock using collections of similar objects – e.g., leaves, pebbles, feathers

4 Keep your sections aligned in the minutes of the clock

Mental health and wellbeing

INSIDE

OCD

- Identify what OCD is, develop our knowledge of how it affects people, and explore what can impact it.

Obsessive compulsive disorder (OCD) is a particularly misunderstood mental health condition. Perceptions have not been helped by television programmes that ridicule those with obsessive compulsions, such as cleaning or handwashing. The condition is as its name implies, regular and obsessive thoughts, leading to compulsive actions and behaviours, to try to soothe the anxiety that manifests. These are often referred to as *rituals* and the obsessive thoughts as *intrusive* thoughts. For example, one may have a repeated obsessive thought around germs and contamination and therefore may be compelled to only eat food they have prepared themselves. OCD can be debilitating and can feel shameful for those who suffer with it. Understanding, empathy, and tolerance go a long way to making those people feel more comfortable with their condition. This session serves to introduce OCD, define what it is, and tackle some of the common misconceptions around it.

You will need:

- Whiteboard and marker
- Internet access
- Individual ICT access
- Exercise books
- OCD myth/fact sheet
- General art and creative resources

1 Starter

Write up 'OCD' on the whiteboard. What does OCD stand for? Once the words have been identified (obsessive compulsive disorder) then use scaffolded questioning to draw out ideas on what your group thinks it may mean.

2 Read and define

At the time of writing, Young Minds provide an excellent page of information on their website explaining what OCD is (internet search: 'young minds OCD'). Have a read yourself before the session and decide how long it will take your group to read the information. Set them a task of doing this and then pull them back together as a group to discuss and agree on a collective definition of OCD to write into their books.

3 OCD myth and fact

There are many myths about OCD and, on page 129, you will find a sheet containing ten different statements about OCD. Your group must decide which ones are myths and which ones are fact. It is a bit unfair, as all of them are myths, but it is interesting to see how many of them pick up on this. If anyone asks you, be blasé and say something like 'if that's what you think then tick them all as myths' so as not to give anything away. Give them a time limit to work though and then pull the group back together and discuss.

4 Group OCD poster/display

Your group must collaborate to produce a poster or display that tackles the myths around OCD. Allocate the following roles out to the group (obviously multiply up the myths if working in a smaller group):

- Layout/design.
- Writing and providing a definition of OCD.
- Visuals/images.
- Each of the ten myths.

Depending on the overall engagement of your group, you could assign this as an individual task, rather than a group one.

Mental health and wellbeing

OUTSIDE

Fashion a feather

- Feathers are incredible. They are such an important and awesome part of a bird – why not design your own!

Feathers are awesome – they are the ultimate multipurpose appendage! The base layer of feathers, or 'down', is soft and fluffy, acting as an insulating layer to keep birds warm. Obviously, wing and tail feathers are used for flying. Wing feathers are arranged in overlapping layers that fan out to create that aerodynamic wing shape. The feathers on a bird's body are also designed to smooth out into streamlined flight patterns, or contours. Think of a Peacock, or a Bird of Paradise – both have gaudy, attention-seeking plumages that are used to attract the opposite sex. Some birds have such cryptic feather patterns that they are cleverly camouflaged into their habitats. Not only are they brilliant and useful parts of a bird, but, as I said, they are also awesome and so this activity celebrates this fact. By now, you should hopefully have designed a duck and blinged up a butterfly; now it is time to fashion a feather!

You will need:

- Feather outline sheet
- Access to an outdoor space

1 Head outside

This activity is a bit of fun.

2 Fashion-a-feather

Gather up loads of natural materials such as twigs, leaves, grass, conkers, acorns etc., and then you can use the feather outline sheet on page 130 simply for guidance, or you could print it off on A3 paper to use as an actual outline; either way, use the natural materials to design and decorate your own feather. This can also be facilitated as an indoor activity with arts and crafts materials, too – it works well both ways.

Mental health and wellbeing

Here is a beautiful selection of feathers from my friend, natural history writer, Jon Dunn. Clockwise from top left: Waxwing, Jay, Barn Owl, Bittern.

Mental health and wellbeing

INSIDE

Stress

- Develop awareness of what stress is and how we respond to it as individuals.

In modern society, there are many things that cause stress to adults and, being from older generations, we may perceive that the stresses on adolescents pale in significance when compared to 'our' issues, like housing, debt, employment, and the cost of living. The two biggest causes of stress in adolescence are school and then social interactions, particularly those on social media. Things that shape and set us up for those adult stressors. Stress is natural. It is our body's chemical response to pressure and threat and can be useful in helping us to perform under pressure and achieve our goals. Too much stress, however, can have a negative impact on our physical and mental health, and it is important that we are able to reflect on the things that cause us stress, regardless of our age. This session gives an overview of what stress is, what causes it biologically, what makes us stressed, and encourages us to reflect on it in several ways.

You will need:

- Slideshow
- Whiteboard and marker
- Stress trumps sheet
- Exercise books

1 Introductory discussion and sticky notes activity

Ask your group what they think stress is? Discuss and then define. Look at the definition on slide 17 and copy into books. Draw the outline of a person on the whiteboard. All group members to write down something that they do or that happens to them when they are stressed. Stick these sticky notes both around and within the outline. You can also hand out the person outline on page 121 for your group members to annotate, or simply take a photo of the board to print and then stick into books.

2 Locus of control

Get your group to all draw two circles in their books, a small one inside a larger one. The inner one must be labelled as 'things I can control' and the outer as 'things I can't control'. Give them 5 minutes to fill their circle diagrams in. When the time is up, draw the same circles onto the board and collate each person's thoughts to make a group version. Discuss any key points/trends that arise.

3 Group discussion

Ask each group member and any support staff to think of a time when they were stressed. Reiterate that this is a safe environment for sharing and encourage the sharing of the experience. I recommend that you or a member of support staff go first and model this. The key questions here are what did it feel like and what were the signs and symptoms of stress in your experience?

4 Stress trumps

The final activity is a bit of creative fun – making your own top trumps cards based on different causes of stress. First, facilitate a discussion identifying things that can cause stress. On page 131, you will find a template of a top trumps card with five categories for the scoring system, each to be scored out of 100. The impact score is how many people in the population are affected by it (most will be 100), collaboration is subjective as to whether you think you can work with others to tackle the issue, health is the impact it has on all elements of your health, combat is how much you can do something about it, and the stress trumps score is an average of the other four scores. Ultimately, this activity is a bit of fun, although it does help to tackle and embed a potentially sensitive topic:

- Top box – write the name of the issue that causes stress.
- Second box – draw or find an image to represent the cause of stress.
- Third box – the five categories for scoring the card.

Mental health and wellbeing

OUTSIDE

Regulation – outdoors

- A selection of basic mindfulness/meditative activities that can be facilitated in an outdoor space.

We have already touched on the wider concept of mindfulness in this book, particularly with activities that utilise grounding techniques, such as the sonic sit-spot. But what exactly *is* mindfulness? Rooted in Buddhist meditative approaches, mindfulness is simply allowing ourselves to become more attuned to the present moment, paying attention non-judgementally, with the goal of reducing stress. It was coined in 1979 by Doctor Jon Kabat-Zinn, an American microbiologist, who devised an eight-week stress reduction programme that formed the roots of a wider approach to wellbeing (Mindful staff editors at Mindful.org, 2022). It seems to have exploded in popularity since the 1990s, becoming part of the NHS's mental health treatment and prevention regime and saturating the retail sector with mindfulness 'products', such as colouring books. Mindfulness makes complete sense to be practised outdoors. To fully appreciate the outdoors and nature, we must slow down our minds and embrace places with all our senses, as encouraged in many of the outdoor activities in this book. Therefore, the three regulation techniques in this activity are to be practised in an outdoor space; head out, and get your group members to find their individual sit-spots then facilitate and practise each of the strategies while outdoors.

You will need:

- Access to an outdoor space

1 STOP

This is a simple four-step process to take stock of what is happening to your mind and body during stress. First, encourage the group to try and guess what the acronym stands for, which is – Stop, Take a breath, Observe, and Proceed. Be clear that this is easier said than done and takes practice. Focus on using the breath to pause and think about what is happening. It is during this brief thinking time that we can notice the physiological effects of stress and that we are about to respond in a negative manner. Becoming aware is the first step to being able to tackle this.

2 Finger tracing

This is an excellent tactile mindfulness technique for grounding in times of stress. Explain that when you feel stress/anger rising, you can stop and place your forefinger on the base of your thumb. Slowly trace the shape of your thumb and all your fingers as you breathe in and out. This can be done covertly or overtly, but is a good way to try and regulate in the moment.

3 Body scan

The body scan is a key practice in mindfulness, and an easy one to teach to young people, if they are willing to approach it with an open mind, as it can be funny! It is a simple exercise and encourages awareness of the body and being present in the moment. Here's a guide on how to facilitate it:

- Lie down on your back on a comfortable surface and close your eyes.
- Breathe in through your nose and out through your mouth, slowly, until you fall into a deep rhythm of breathing.
- Tense every muscle in your body as tightly as you can.
- Squish/curl your toes and feet, squeeze your hands into fists, and make your legs and arms as hard and solid as you can; hold it for as long as it is comfortable to do so.
- Release all your muscles and relax for a few minutes.
- Discuss and reflect on how your body felt throughout the body scan.
- Repeat, with growing focus and awareness.

Mental health and wellbeing

INSIDE

An active mind

- Explore the benefits of having a hobby and relate this to concept of the five ways to wellbeing.

In most guidance suggesting ways that you can boost your wellbeing, we are told that taking up a hobby can be beneficial. In this activity, we look at hobbies through the lens of the five ways to wellbeing, which are a framework of five things we can bring into our lives to enhance our wellbeing, that is, to be active, learn, give, take notice, and connect. Most hobbies can be interwoven within these five elements and I dare say that the more of the five that a hobby enhances your life, then the better that hobby is for your overall wellbeing. Hobbies can bring rewards and rewards can release dopamine (the chemical that makes you feel good) but keeping your mind active with a hobby does not just make you feel good. Evidence shows that engaging with a hobby can slow the rate of hippocampal atrophy associated with Alzheimer's and other dementias. This activity takes a step back and looks at a range of hobbies from a wellbeing perspective, encouraging reflection on activities that your group may not correlate could be good for them.

You will need:

- Whiteboard and marker
- Slideshow
- Exercise books
- Hobby cards sheet
- ICT access

Cut out the hobby cards before the session and keep together ready.

1 *Discussion with visual*

Show slide 18, containing a brief introduction to the five ways to wellbeing, without naming what the five ways are. Then move onto slide 19, which is a visual depiction of the five 'ways' – do not say what they are and encourage the group to guess what each image represents. From L-R, they are to learn, to take notice, to be active, to connect, and to give.

2 Deeper discussion and categorising activity

Ask the group to draw a five-column-table in their books with each one of the five ways as a column title. Then facilitate a collaborative discussion to identify as many ways as possible in which we could bring each area into our lives. For example, for to connect, we could join a club.

3 Open question before the next activity

Are there any activities/hobbies that you can think of that could cover or involve all five of the five ways to wellbeing?

4 Discussion and card sorting

Gather the group around one table (with a larger group you will have to approach this in a different way, perhaps individually) and put the hobby cards from page 32 on the table. Go through them and discuss what each one is (there are some weird ones in there). Discussion questions: are they all positive activities (yes) and are they all cool (yes, indeed!). Discuss how to map the five ways to wellbeing across each one and display the parkour example on slide 20 to the group. Group members are to then choose five hobbies from the hobby cards, and write them into their books, mapping the five ways to wellbeing to their chosen hobbies as shown in the parkour example.

5 Independent extension activity

Choose your own hobby or something that you like doing and create a persuasive factsheet for it, using images and text, and featuring the five ways to wellbeing and how they tie in with it. This can be done by hand and/or with internet-sourced images and information.

Mental health and wellbeing

OUTSIDE

Nature calm jars

- A final creative activity, making our own 'calm jars' using natural materials.

There is a lot of research out there stating that the swirling shapes and patterns of (what we would define as) a snow globe, can help dysregulated children to self-soothe. These tend to be packaged up under the name of 'calm jars'. None of the information seems particularly scientific, but there are several big players in the media and psychology spheres who support the concept. Essentially, shaking up the contents of the jar and then focusing on the swirling then settling items suspended in it provides something specific and separate to focus on, unaffected by external stressors. Biodegradable glitter is an excellent filler as it can catch the light at different angles, creating hypnotic patterns and 'worlds' in the jar. Most of the time these are made using glitter glue and water, but I thought it would be awesome to make them from using colourful, found natural items suspended in water instead – which has the bonus of making the water change colour. If you really want to, you can use glycerine to slow the objects down, but a clear craft glue works just as well. I used a jam jar at home, but it is much easier and safer to use 500ml plastic bottles, plus it also promotes recycling.

You will need:

- A clear receptacle as noted above
- Access to an outdoor space with a range of natural items
- Water
- Glycerine (or craft glue as noted above)
- Biodegradable glitter if you choose to add this

1 Head outside

Go to the nearest available outdoor space. This does not need to be ultra-biodiverse but that will give you a greater range of natural resources to find.

Mental health and wellbeing

2 Gather!

Gather up a range of colourful natural materials such as flowers, leaves, seeds, conkers, acorns etc. These will form the contents of your natural calm jar. As you can see from my images, the brighter and more varied, the better! You will need to gather enough to fill at least a quarter of your chosen receptacle. Do not assume that the season will have a negative impact on your ability to find natural treasures; I found the items in my images during late autumn.

3 Fill it up!

You will most likely want to take the materials in and fill the jars up indoors, as you will need access to water to put inside the calm jar. You simply fill three-quarters of the jar with water and the remaining quarter with either glycerine or clear craft glue; you can also add your biodegradable glitter at this point if you choose to (traditional glitter is not biodegradable). Give the contents one big shake and allow to settle. This settling process is what you can then watch to help regulate and refocus yourself.

References

Arain, M., Haque, M., Johal, L., Mathur, P., Nel, W., Rais, A., Sandhu, R. & Sharma, Sushil (2013). Maturation of the Adolescent Brain. *Neuropsychiatric Disease and Treatment*, 9, 449–461.

Bakolis, I., Hammoud, R., Smythe, M., Gibbons, J., Davidson, N., Tognin, S. & Mechelli, A. (2018). Urban Mind: Using Smartphone Technologies to Investigate the Impact of Nature on Mental Well-being in Real Time. *BioScience*, 68(2), 134–145.

Balmford, A., Clegg, L., Coulson, T. & Taylor, J. (2002). Why Conservationists Should Heed Pokémon. *Science*, 295, 2367.

Barrable, A. & Booth, D. (2020) Increasing Nature Connection in Children: A Mini Review of Interventions. *Front. Psychol.*, 11, 492.

Bird, W. (2007) *Natural Thinking: A Report Investigating the Links between the Natural Environment, Biodiversity and Mental Health*, 1st ed. Royal Society for the Protection of Birds, London.

Bruce, C. (2010). *Emotional Literacy in the Early Years*. SAGE Publications, London.

Chavaly, D. & Naachimuthu, K. (2020). Human Nature Connection and Mental Health: What Do We Know So Far? *Indian Journal of Health and Well-being*, 11(1–3), 84–92.

Cherniss, C., Extein, M., Goleman, D. & Weissberg, R. (2006). Emotional Intelligence: What Does the Research Really Indicate? *Educational Psychologist*, 41(4), 239–245.

Coppock, V. (2007). It's Good to Talk! A Multidimensional Qualitative Study of the Effectiveness of Emotional Literacy Work in Schools. *Children & Society*, 21(6), 405–419.

DfE (2018). *Mental Health and Behaviour in Schools: Departmental Advice for School Staff*. Department for Education, London. Crown Copyright.

DfE (2019). *Relationships Education, Relationships and Sex Education (RSE) and Health Education Statutory Guidance for Governing Bodies, Proprietors, Head Teachers, Principals, Senior Leadership Teams, Teachers*. Department for Education, London. Crown Copyright.

DfE (2022). *Keeping Children Safe in Education 2022: Statutory Guidance for Schools and Colleges*. Department for Education, London. Crown Copyright.

DfE & Public Health England (2021). *Guidance: Promoting Children and Young People's Mental Health and Wellbeing: Guidance on the Eight Principles of a Whole School or College Approach to Promoting Mental Health and Wellbeing*. DfE and Public Health England, London. Crown Copyright.

References

Durlak, J., Dymnicki, A., Schellinger, A., Taylor, R. & Weissberg, R. (2011). The Impact of Enhancing Students' Social and Emotional Learning: A Meta-Analysis of School-Based Universal Interventions. *Child Development*, 82(1), 405–432.

Fiennes, C., Oliver, E., Dickson, K., Escobar, D., Romans, A. & Oliver, S. (2015). *The Existing Evidence-Base about the Effectiveness of Outdoor Learning*. UCL, Institute for Outdoor Learning, Blagrave Trust and Giving Evidence.

Humphrey, N., Lendrum, A. & Wigelsworth, M. (2010). *Social and Emotional Aspects of Learning (SEAL) Programme in Secondary Schools: National Evaluation*. DfE and School of Education, University of Manchester, Manchester.

Kilmann Diagnostics LLC (2009–2023). *Take the Thomas-Kilmann Instrument | Improve How You Resolve Conflict.* https://kilmanndiagnostics.com/overview-thomas-kilmann-conflict-mode-instrument-tki/How You Resolve Conflict (kilmanndiagnostics.com).

Klerk, M. & Jung Society of Utah (2015). Mandalas: Symbols of the Self. Available at https://jungutah.org/blog/mandalas-symbols-of-the-self-2/.

Louv, R. (2010). *Last Child in the Woods*. Atlantic Books.

Low, S.M. (1992). 'Symbolic Ties That Bind' in I. Altman & S.M. Low (eds.), Place Attachment. *Human Behavior and Environment, Advances in Theory and Research*, 12, at https://doi.org/10.1007/978-1-4684-8753-4_8.

Mann, J., Gray, T., Truong, S., Brymer, E., Passy, R., Ho, S., Sahlberg, P., Ward, K., Bentsen, P., Curry, C. & Cowper, R. (2022). Getting Out of the Classroom and Into Nature: A Systematic Review of Nature-Specific Outdoor Learning on School Children's Learning and Development. *Front Public Health*. May 16, 10.

Mannion, G., Fenwick, A., Nugent, C. & I'Anson, J. (2011). Teaching in Nature. Scottish Natural Heritage Commission Report No. 476.

Mayer, J.D., DiPaolo, M. & Salovey, P. (1990). Perceiving Affective Content in Ambiguous Visual Stimuli: A Component of Emotional Intelligence. *J Pers Assess*, 54(3–4), 772–781.

Mental Health Foundation (2019). *State of a Generation: Preventing Mental Health Problems in Children and Young People*. Mental Health Foundation, London.

Mental Health Foundation (2022). About Mental Health. Available at https://www.mentalhealth.org.uk/explore-mental-health/about-mental-health.

Mind Tools Content Team (2022). *Mehrabian's Communication Model: Learning to Communicate Clearly.* https://www.mindtools.com/ao9kek8/mehrabians-communication-model.

Mindful staff editors at Mindful.org (2022). Everyday Mindfulness with Jon Kabat-Zinn. Available at https://www.mindful.org/everyday-mindfulness-with-jon-kabat-zinn/.

NHS (2019). Anxiety in Children. Available at https://www.nhs.uk/mental-health/children-and-young-adults/advice-for-parents/anxiety-in-children/. Crown Copyright.

References

NHS Digital (2022). Mental Health of Children and Young People Surveys: Mental Health of Children and Young People in England 2022 – wave 3 follow up to the 2017 survey. Available at https://digital.nhs.uk/data-and-information/publications/statistical/mental-health-of-children-and-young-people-in-england/2022-follow-up-to-the-2017-survey.

NSPCC (2022). Safeguarding d/Deaf and disabled Children and Young People: Guidance on Protecting d/Deaf and Disabled Children and Young People from abuse. Available at https://learning.nspcc.org.uk/safeguarding-child-protection/deaf-and-disabled-children.

OFSTED (2008). Learning Outside the Classroom. How Far Should You Go? Ofsted, London. Crown Copyright.

Pfeifer, J.H. & Berkman, E.T. (2018). The Development of Self and Identity in Adolescence: Neural Evidence and Implications for a Value-Based Choice Perspective on Motivated Behavior. *Child Dev Perspect*, 2(3), 158–164.

Pickering, S. (2017). *Teaching Outdoors Creatively* (Learning to Teach in the Primary School Series). Routledge, London.

Ratcliffe, E., Gatersleben, B. & Sowden, P.T. (2013). Bird Sounds and their Contributions to Perceived Attention Restoration and Stress Recovery. *Journal of Environmental Psychology*, 36, 221–228; https://www.sciencedirect.com/science/article/pii/S0272494413000650.

Sharp, P. (2007). *Nurturing Emotional Literacy: A Practical Guide for Teachers, Parents and Those in the Caring Professions*. David Fulton Publishers, Oxford.

Verhoeven, M., Poorthuis, A.M.G. & Volman, M. (2019). The Role of School in Adolescents' Identity Development. A Literature Review. *Educ. Psychol. Rev.*, 31, 35–63;). https://doi.org/10.1007/s10648-018-9457-3.

Weare, K. & Gray, G. (2003). *What Works in Developing Children's Emotional and Social Competence and Wellbeing?* Department for Education and Skills, London.

World Health Organization (2022). COVID-19 Pandemic Triggers 25% Increase in Prevalence of Anxiety and Depression Worldwide: Wake-up Call to all Countries to Step Up Mental Health Services and Support. Available at https://www.who.int/news/item/02-03-2022-covid-19-pandemic-triggers-25-increase-in-prevalence-of-anxiety-and-depression-worldwide.

WWT (n.d.). Blue Prescribing Project. Available at https://www.wwt.org.uk/our-work/projects/blue-prescribing/.

Young Minds (2021). The Impact of Covid-19 on Young People with Mental Health Needs. Available at https://www.youngminds.org.uk/about-us/reports-and-impact/coronavirus-impact-on-young-people-with-mental-health-needs/.

Appendices

The Feelings Triangle

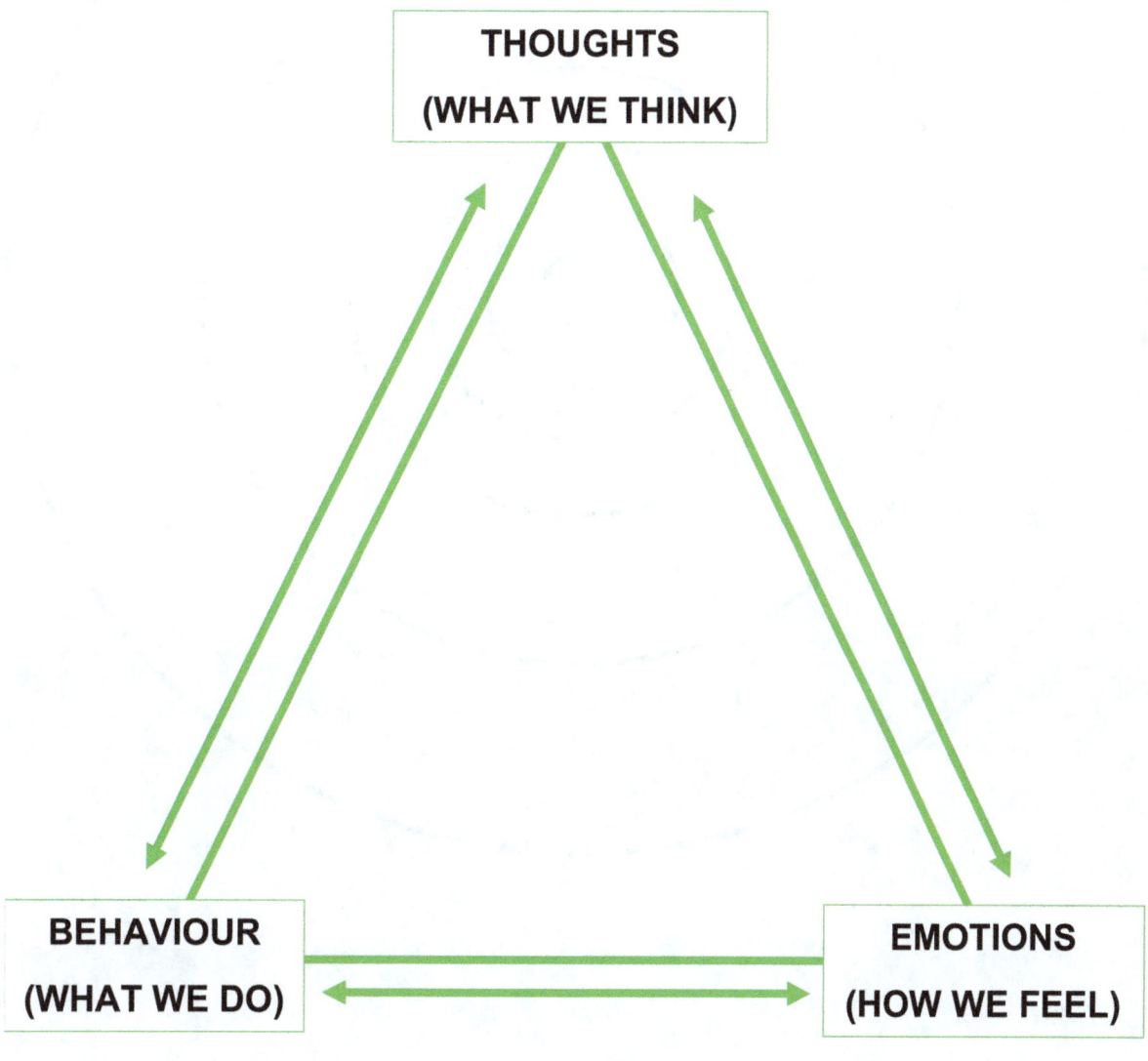

Appendices

Sonar Map

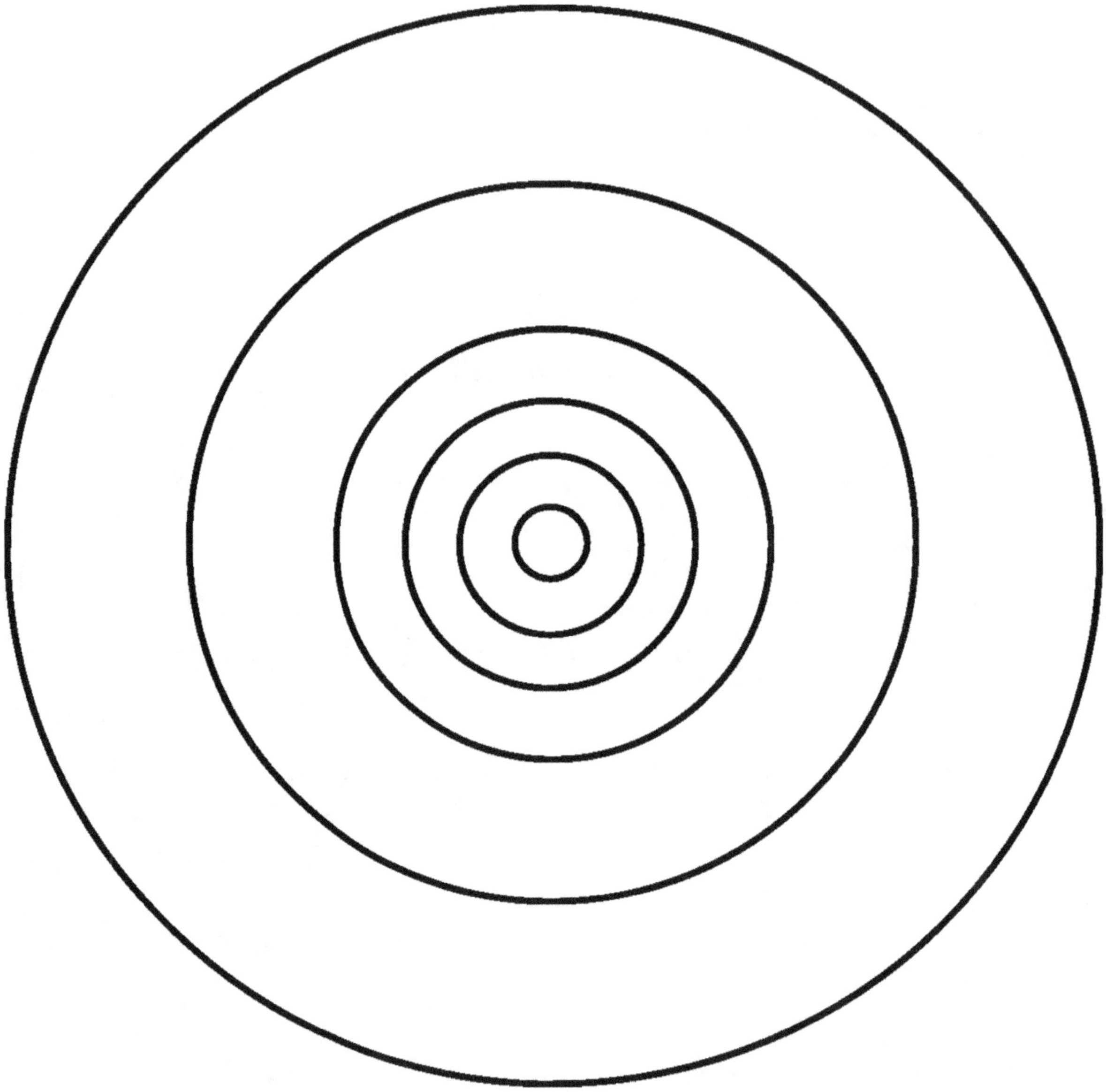

Appendices

The Escalation Curve

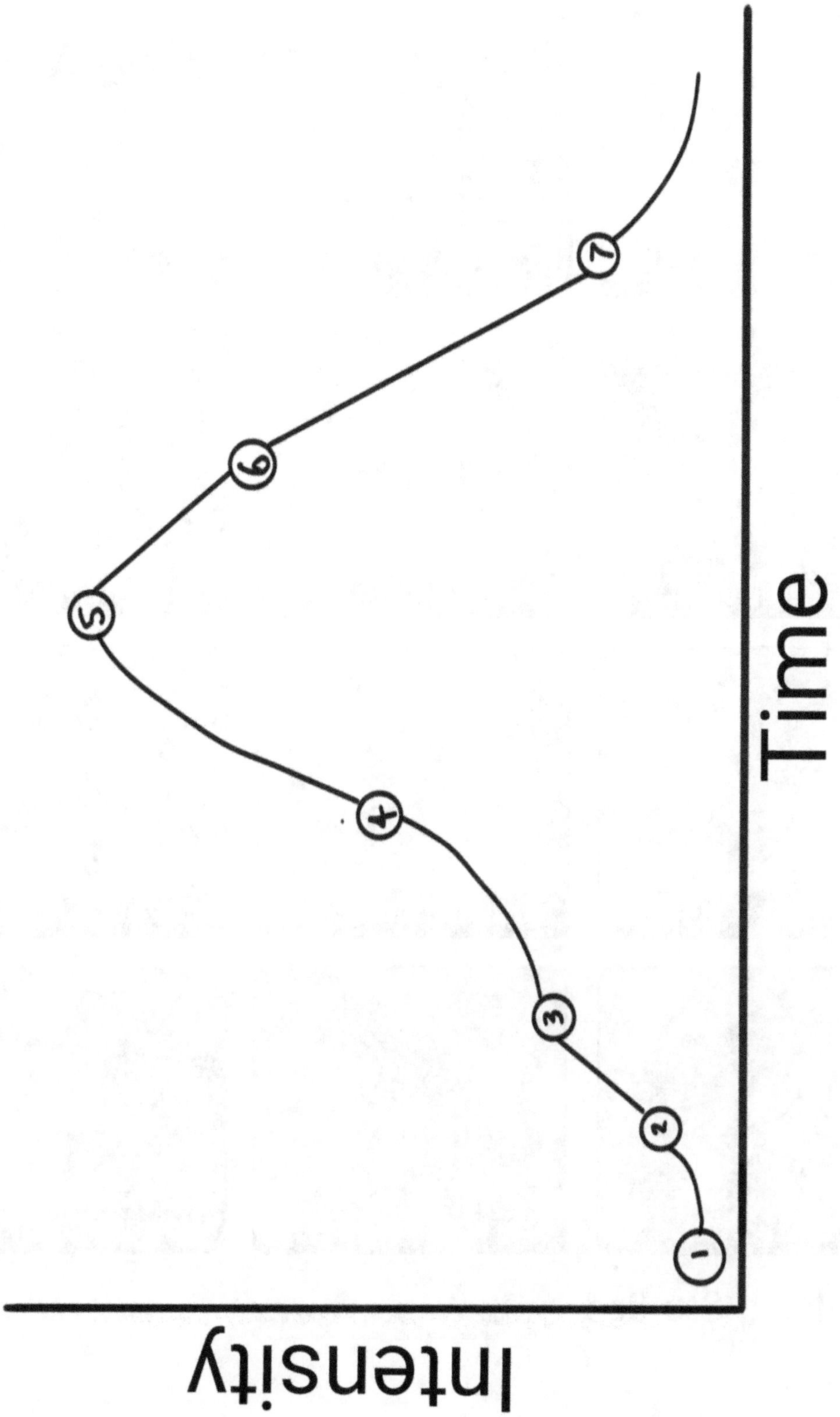

Copyright material from Joe Harkness (2024), *Inside/Outside*, Routledge

Appendices

School ground birds....

Blackbird	 Blue Tit	 Chaffinch
 Collared Dove	 Dunnock	 Goldfinch
 Great Tit	 House Sparrow	 Magpie
 Robin	 Starling	 Wood Pigeon

Created by R. Farley-Brown, FSC Publications © Field Studies Council 2022
This may be copied for educational use.

Copyright material from Joe Harkness (2024), *Inside/Outside*, Routledge

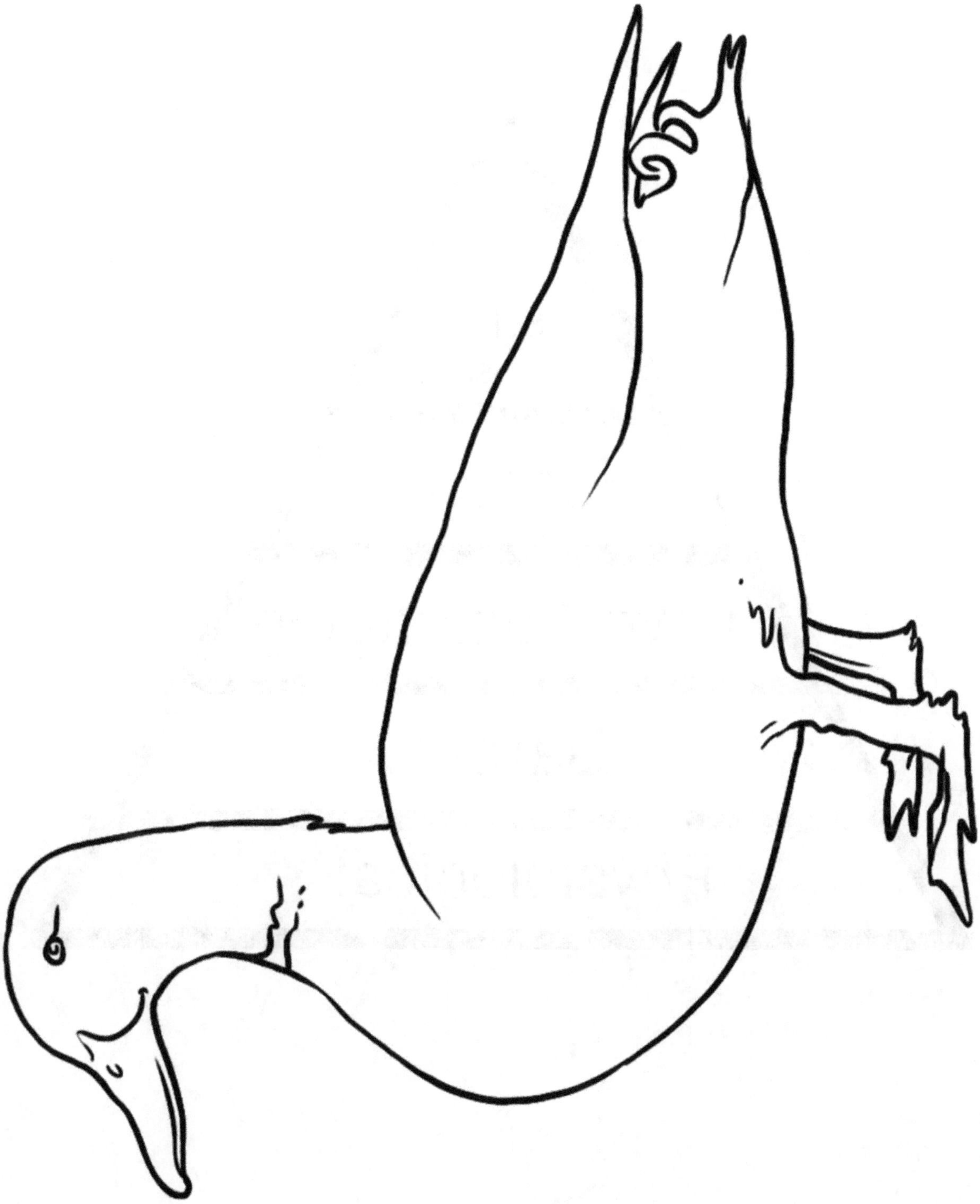

Appendices

Appendices

Maslow's Hierarchy of Needs

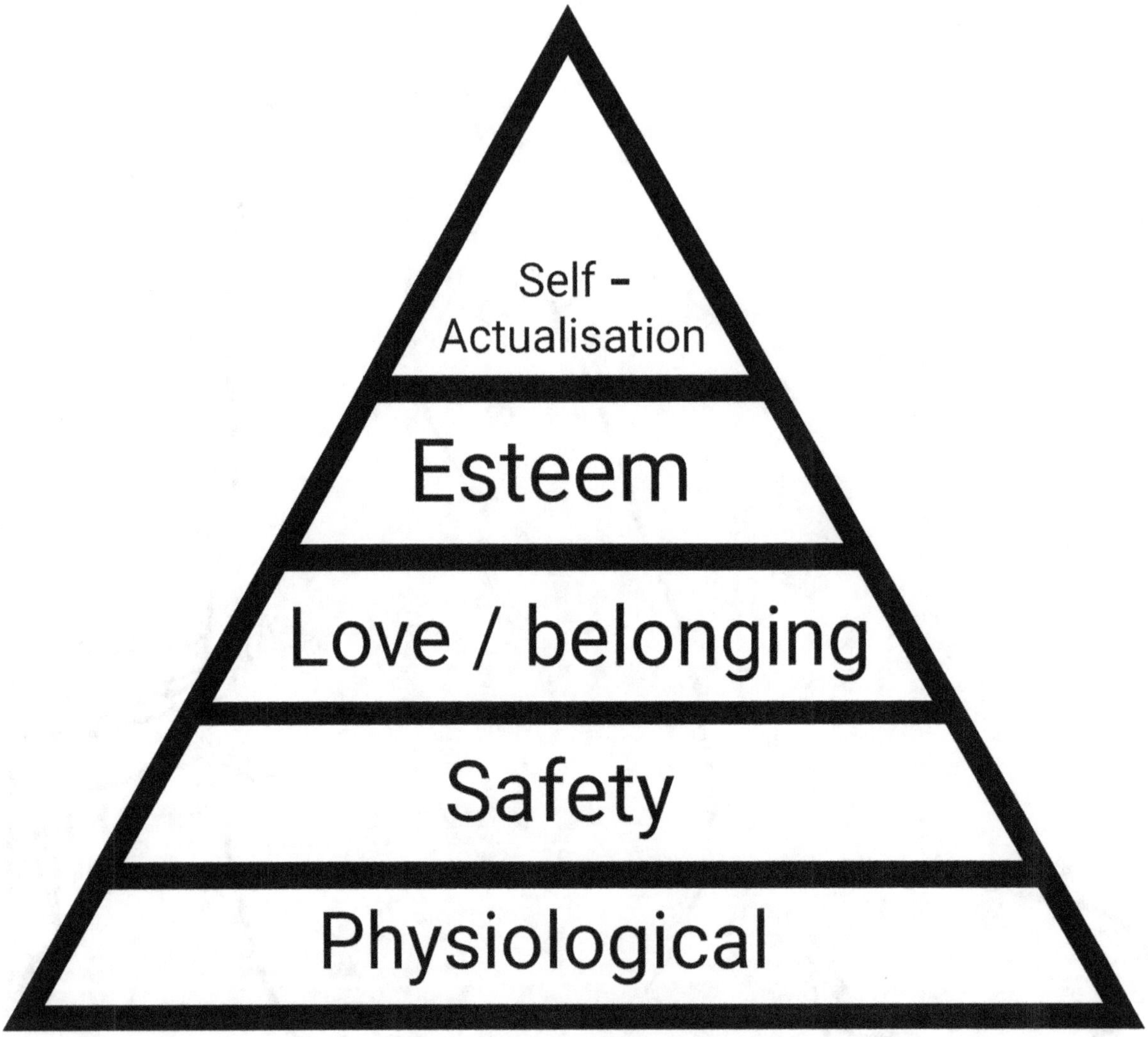

- Self-Actualisation
- Esteem
- Love / belonging
- Safety
- Physiological

Appendices

Maslow in school

Need	How is it met in school
Physiological	
Safety	
Love and belonging	
Esteem	
Self-actualisation	

Appendices

Paint Swatches

Appendices

The Top-10 UK Fears and Phobias (according to various sources)

1. Glossophobia
2. Acrophobia
3. Agoraphobia
4. Claustrophobia
5. Latrophobia
6. Arachnophobia
7. Thalassophobia
8. Coulrophobia
9. Aerophobia
10. Ophidiophobia

But what do you think they are fears and phobias of?

1.
2.
3.
4.
5.
6.
7.
8.
9.
10.

What scares you?

1. My biggest fear is…
2. The scariest thing that's ever happened to me is…
3. I faced a fear when…
4. The ingredients for a scary film or story are…

Copyright material from Joe Harkness (2024), *Inside/Outside*, Routledge

Appendices

School ground mini beasts....

Woodlouse	Earthworm	Slug
Garden Snail	Bumblebee	Hoverfly
Beetle	Ladybird	Shieldbug
Millipede	Ant	Spider

Created by R. Farley-Brown, FSC Publications © Field Studies Council 2022
This may be copied for educational use.

Copyright material from Joe Harkness (2024), *Inside/Outside*, Routledge

Appendices

Clench your fists	Say something horrible	Punch walls
Pace up and down	Struggle to make decisions	Start sweating
Shout or scream	Throw something	Overthink
Run away	Stare aggressively	Deny responsibility
Cry	Raise your voice	Panic
Breathe quickly	Shutdown	Become fidgety
Laugh	Tremor/shake	Make a joke out of it

Appendices

Signs of Anger

The anger cycle

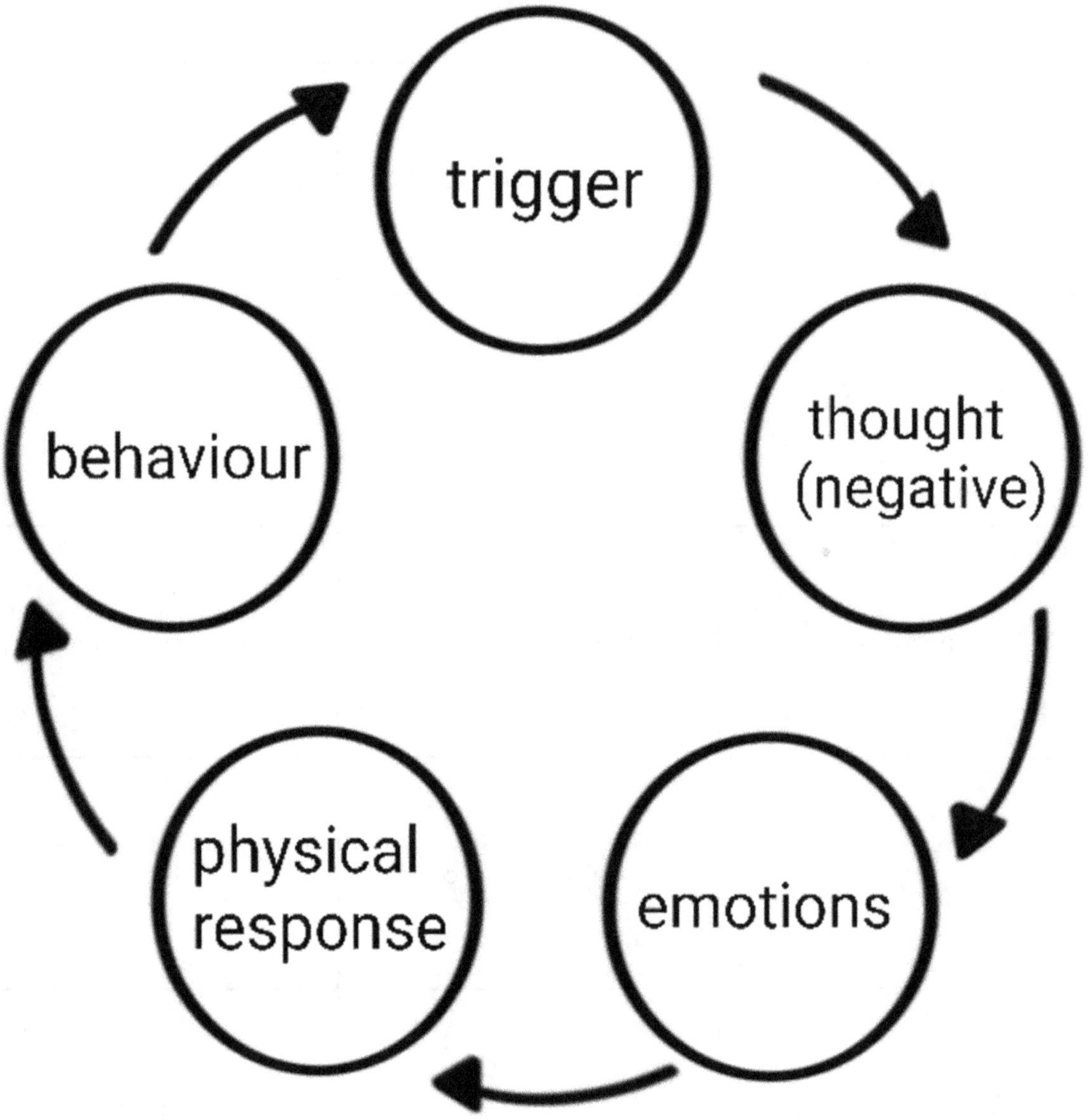

- trigger
- thought (negative)
- emotions
- physical response
- behaviour

Appendices

Sensory Sit-spot

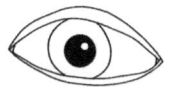

Appendices

Gratitude Scavenger Hunt

FIND …	
	A colourful flower
	Something that makes you smile
	A leaf shaped like a random animal
	Something which smells amazing
	Your favourite tree
	Something which is your favourite colour
	A space you like to sit in
	Something that makes a beautiful sound
	An object which has multiple uses
	Something a friend would like
	Something which is nice to touch
	Something utterly beautiful
	Something really green
	Something which reminds you of home
	Something or somewhere that feels warm
	The quietest spot you can find

Appendices

Texture Bingo

ROUGH	SLIMY	CRUNCHY	VELVETY
SOFT	COARSE	FLUFFY	SLIMEY
SPONGY	FUZZY	GRAINY	SPIKY
HAIRY	DUSTY	BUMPY	FIRM

Copyright material from Joe Harkness (2024), *Inside/Outside*, Routledge

Appendices

Identity Tree Instructions
Part 1

Using sticky notes, cut-out shapes, illustrations, or anything else creative as leaves, complete your identity tree by answering the following questions **on** the leaves:

1. Which people are important to me? (Family/friends/role models, etc.)
2. Which places are important to me? (My area, city, my/my family's country, etc.)
3. Which beliefs, values or ideas are important to me? (Religious, non-religious, political etc.)
4. What is my personality like? (Kind, creative, funny etc.)
5. What do I do well and enjoy doing?
6. What do I look like?
7. What am I studying/ What job do I want to do/what job do I do?
8. What gender am I? What is my sexuality?
9. What groups do I belong to?
10. What are my hopes for your future? (What type of life do I want? What type of person do I want to be?)

Part 2

Part 2 is about thinking where our identity comes from. Is it family, friends, community, culture, religion, the media, books, a life experience, education, a role model/influential person, genes, social norms etc.?

Try to complete the following sentences in the roots of your identity tree:

1. My religion/beliefs/values come from...
2. My personality comes from...
3. My hobbies come from...
4. My strengths and skills come from...
5. My appearance/style comes from...
6. My dreams for the future come from...
7. The person/people I look up to is/are...

Appendices

Our Habitats

Appendices

Signs of Sustainability

Appendices

Person Outline

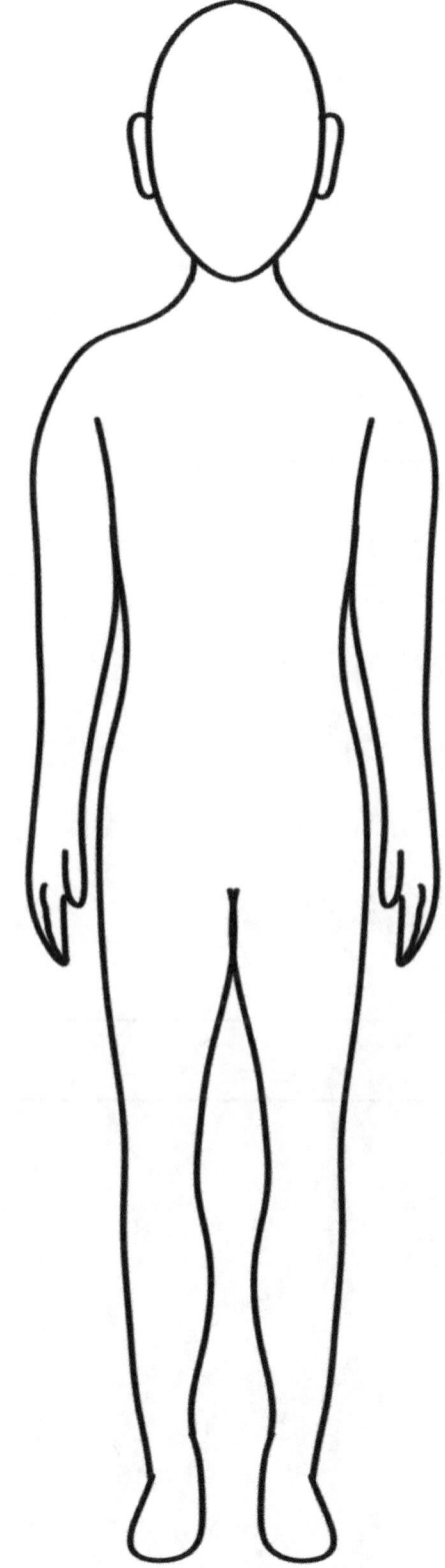

Copyright material from Joe Harkness (2024), *Inside/Outside*, Routledge

Appendices

Realising Respect

Appendices

School ground plants...

Daisy	 Buttercup	 Dandelion
 Red Clover	 White Clover	 Speedwell
 Selfheal	 Red Dead Nettle	 Mouse-ear
 Pineapple Mayweed	 Short mown grass	 Long flowering grass

Created by R. Farley-Brown, FSC Publications © Field Studies Council 2022
This may be copied for educational use.

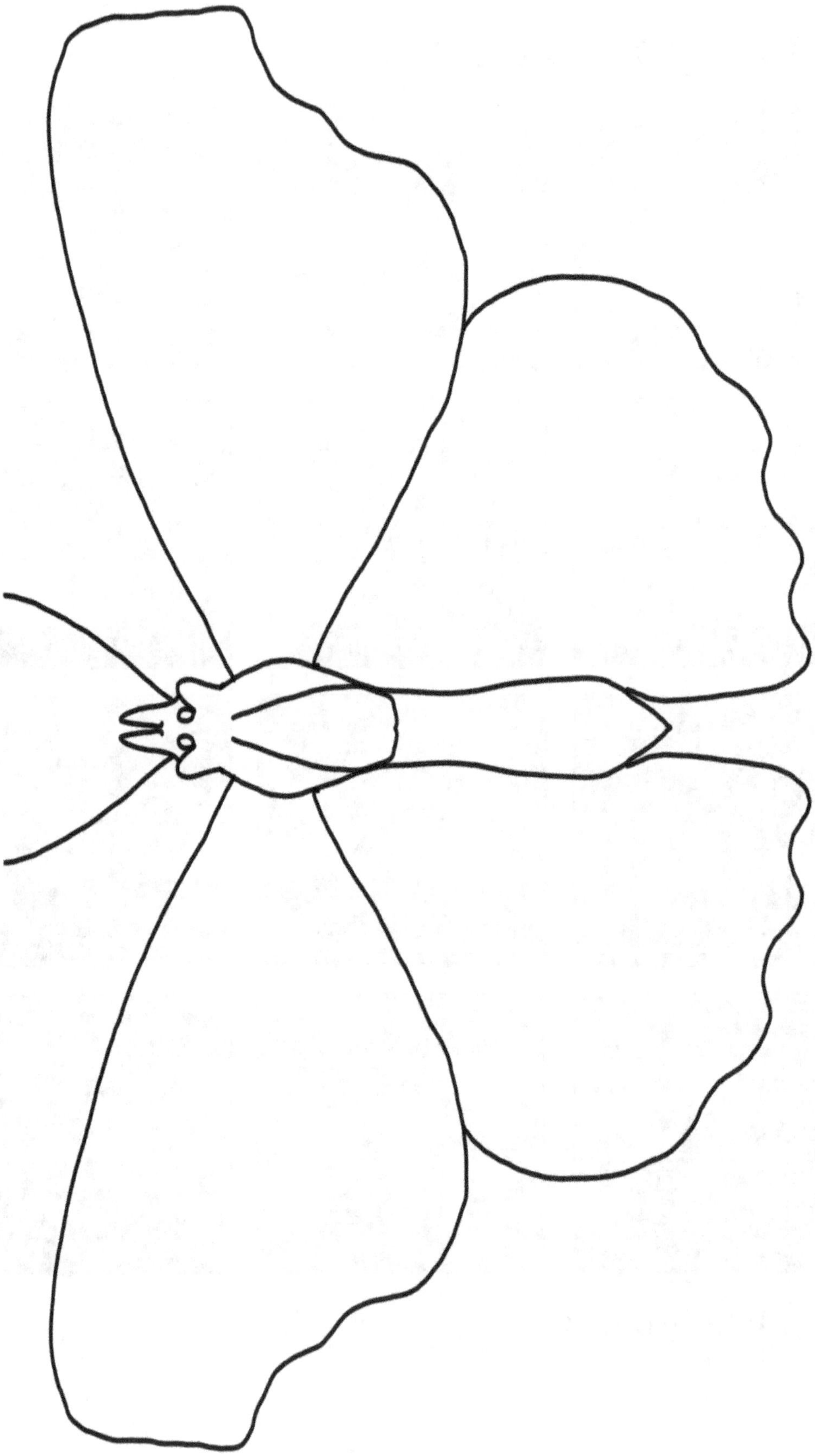

Appendices

Mental Health Scenarios

Your friend keeps posting pictures in the group chat of her self-harming. They're cutting the inside of their thigh with a pencil sharpener blade, in neat thin lines and then sharing them with everyone, saying they're feeling 'so depressed with this world.' What could you do?
Your friend won't come out at break and lunch anymore. They spend most of it in the school safe space and then come out to go back to their lessons. You've tried asking them why they won't come out with you and all they've said is that they want to be alone and don't feel comfortable around people now. What could you do?
Your friend is really freaking out about their upcoming GCSE's. They tell you that they were so worried about it the other day that they punched their bedroom wall and pushed their little brother over when he interrupted them revising. What could you do?
Your friend keeps going off to the toilets after eating their lunch with you. When they come out, they often have red eyes and are chewing mint-flavoured come. You are worried that they may be making themselves sick after eating. What could you do?
Your friend has been avoiding PE for ages. They say that they don't want to get changed in front of other people as they feel fat and disgusting in front of other people. They've been wearing a massive coat, too, whatever the weather. What could you do?

Copyright material from Joe Harkness (2024), *Inside/Outside*, Routledge

Appendices

Mental Health Quiz

1. 1 in 9 young people aged 5 to 16 were identified as having a probable mental health problem in 2021.
   False – that's the 2017 figure, it's now 1 in 6 young people.
2. 20% of young people aged 6 to 16 have experienced a deterioration in their mental health since 2017.
   False – the figure is 39.2%
3. All young people with a diagnosable mental health condition in the UK in 2021 has got access to NHS care and treatment.
   False – it's only 1 in 3.
4. 60% of young people asked believed that the pandemic had worsened their mental health.
   False – it's much higher, 83%.
5. A quarter of adult mental health problems are because of adverse childhood experiences.
   False – it's higher at a third.
6. A quarter of young people with identified special educational needs and disability (SEND) have a probable mental disorder.
   False – it's more than half, 56.7%.
7. Half of young people with a probable mental disorder also experience problems with their sleep.
   False – it's much higher at 74.2%.
8. The parents of 50% of young people on the CAMHS (Child and Adolescent Mental Health Service) waiting list reported that their child's mental health had deteriorated whilst waiting.
   False – it's much higher at 76%.
9. Half of young people asked reported that they would much rather access mental health support without visiting their GP.
   False – again, it's higher at 67%.
10. A quarter of those young people stated that they had no idea where else they could go to access support.
    False – you guessed it, it's much higher at over a half, 53%.

Appendices

Depression Wordsearch

The words listed below are all associated with depression and are hidden in the wordsearch. Please try to find them all.

ALONE, ANGRY, ANXIETY, APPETITE, ASHAMED, AVOIDANCE, EMPTY, GUILTY, HARM, HATE, IRRITABLE, ISOLATED, LOW, NUMB, PARANOID, RESTLESS, SADNESS, SLOW, TEARFUL, TIRED, USELESS, WORRY, WORTHLESS

I	R	R	I	T	A	B	L	E	S	X	G	F	S	A
S	A	F	S	O	A	L	E	S	P	U	N	S	I	P
U	M	V	I	S	E	M	E	C	I	U	E	Y	A	P
C	S	W	O	N	E	N	A	L	M	L	F	R	T	E
T	C	E	O	I	D	L	T	B	H	W	A	R	E	T
B	I	L	L	A	D	Y	T	T	F	N	D	O	A	I
E	A	L	S	E	M	A	R	S	O	E	E	W	R	T
D	E	R	I	T	S	O	N	I	E	H	M	O	F	E
W	O	L	S	U	W	S	D	C	B	R	A	A	U	H
D	E	T	A	L	O	S	I	Y	E	L	H	T	L	A
A	N	X	I	E	T	Y	J	E	R	L	S	E	E	R
D	Z	P	C	O	I	X	H	S	B	G	A	P	V	M
P	A	Z	G	A	A	I	F	G	W	H	N	Y	M	H
E	M	P	T	Y	W	I	D	F	R	O	R	A	B	T
J	U	N	J	U	X	F	F	N	D	N	L	P	S	V

Copyright material from Joe Harkness (2024), *Inside/Outside*, Routledge

Appendices

Anxiety Mind-map

WHAT ARE THE SYMPTOMS OF ANXIETY?

Appendices

OCD Myth and Fact

	Myth	Fact
Everyone gets a 'little bit OCD' sometimes		
People with OCD wash their hands all the time		
People with OCD must have all their stuff in alphabetical order		
OCD isn't really that big a deal		
You can't work if you have OCD		
If you're really neat and tidy, you probably have OCD		
Men don't really get OCD		
Kids can't get OCD		
OCD can be a positive		
All OCD compulsions are physical acts that you can see someone doing		

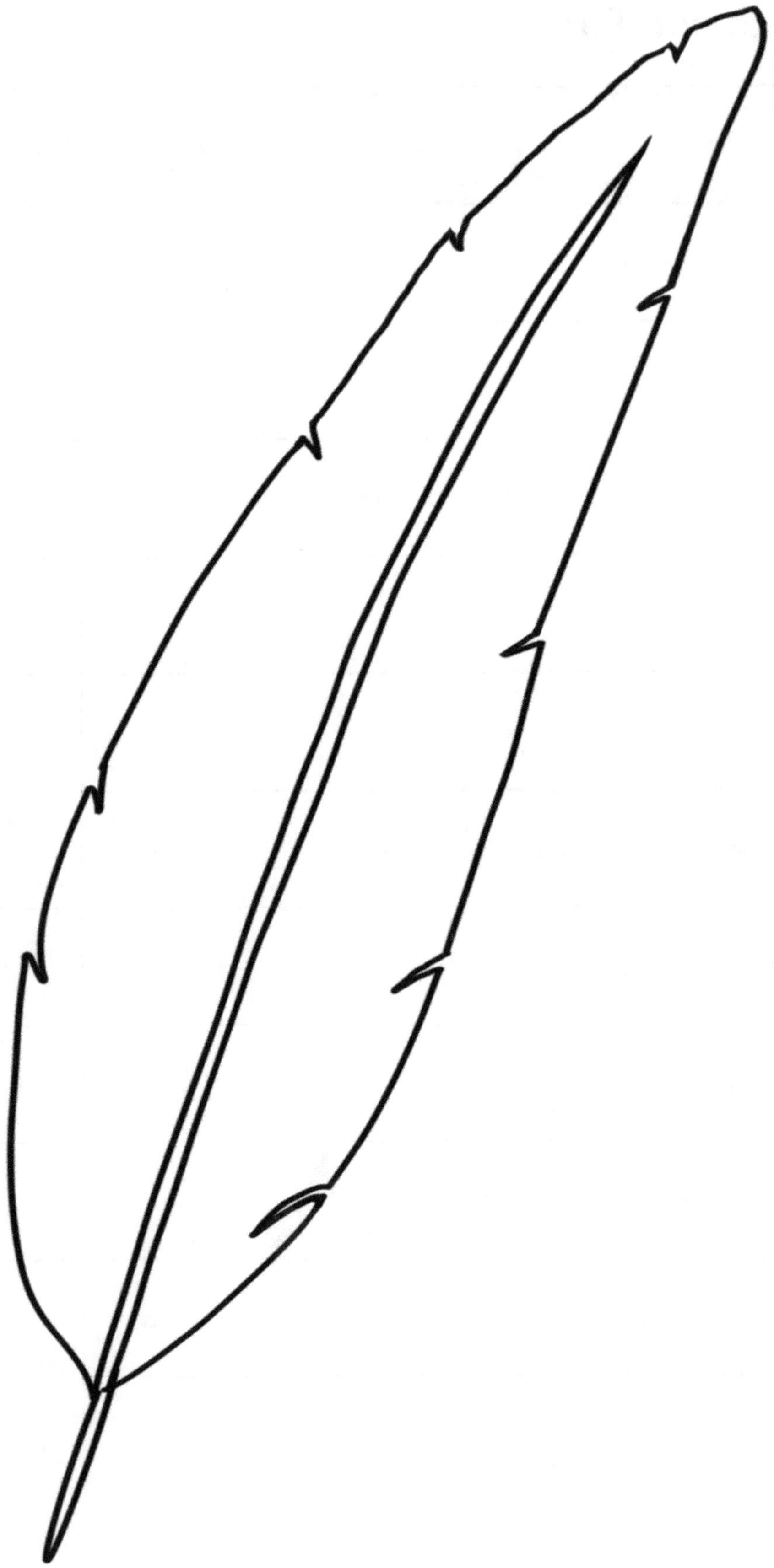

Appendices

Appendices

Stress Trumps Card

Impact	
Collaboration	
Health	
Combat	
Stress trumps	

Copyright material from Joe Harkness (2024), *Inside/Outside*, Routledge

Appendices

Hobby Cards

BIRDWATCHING	WARHAMMER	TAXIDERMY	BOARD GAMING	LARPING	ORIENTEERING
COMIC BOOKS	URBEX	AMATEUR DRAMATICS	POKER	GEOCACHING	PARKOUR
KNITTING	DRONE FLYING	MODEL TRAINS	LIVE STREAMING	SURVIVALISM	WHITTLING
TRAIN SPOTTING	CODING	DUNGEONS AND DRAGONS	TRADING CARDS	HOUSE PLANTS	STAMP COLLECTING
GENEALOGY	METAL DETECTING	BEACH COMBING	ROBOTICS	GEOCACHING	BAKING

Copyright material from Joe Harkness (2024), *Inside/Outside*, Routledge

Index

active mind 96–97
allotments, school 5
alphabet 9; A–Z of noticing nature 78–79
Alzheimer's disease 96
anger 32–33, 113; cycle 33, 114; secondary emotion 33
anxiety 60, 81, 84–85; mind map 128
arts-based activity 47
attention deficit and hyperactivity disorder (ADHD) 6
available, emotionally 11

benefits: of being close to bodies of water 22; of bird watching 18; of birdsong 56; of exposure and immersion in natural sounds 14; of gratitude 38; of improved emotional literacy 4; of nature-specific outdoor learning 5–7
biodiversity 30, 48, 52, 78
birds: birdsong and bird sounds 56–57; design-a-duck 22–23, 107; feathers 90–91, 130; identify and count 18–19, 56, 106; spotting sheet 106; *see also* sonic sit-spot
body language 55; eye contact 63
body scan 95
brain 96; development 11, 41
Buddhism 94
butterflies 68–69, 75, 124

calm jars, nature 98–99
care farming 5
climate change 60
colours, natural 26–27, 34, 110
communication 6, 54–55; non-verbal 55; three 'Vs' of 55
compulsory health education 2, 3
confidence 4, 6
conflict 50–51; Kilmann model of managing 51
coping 20–21; anger 32, 33; happiness 36
COVID-19 pandemic 4
curriculum 11; KS1/2 PSHE 9; KS3/4 PSHE 8

definitions: emotional intelligence 1; emotional literacy 1, 2; sense of place 48

dementia 96
Department for Education (DfE) 2–4, 11
depression 60, 80–81; triangle 81; wordsearch 127
design-a-duck 22–23, 107
discussion 9; shared 'community' approach 9
dopamine 96

emotionally available 11
empathy 2, 9, 28, 41, 50, 58, 62, 88
escalation curve 17, 105
experiential learning 79
explorative learning experiences 46
eye contact 63

fear and phobias 28–29, 111
feathers 90–91, 130
feelings 12–13, 32; triangle 13, 103
fieldwork and field trips 4–5
finger tracing 95
friendships 66–67, 81

general stationery 9
geography: sense of place 48–49
gratitude scavenger hunt 38–39, 116
grounding 15, 56, 57, 74, 94

habitats 52–53, 79, 119
haiku 74–75
happiness 36–37
hobbies 96–97, 132
human geography: sense of place 48–49

ICT-based task 45
identity 46; tree 46–47, 118
insects: counting 30–31, 112; spotting sheet 112
introductory session 10
isolation 4, 81

Jung, C. 86

Kabat-Zinn, J. 94
Key Stages: PSHE curriculum 8, 9

Index

Kilmann, T. 51
kind words 63

listening, mindful 15
loneliness 4, 81

mandalas, nature 86–87
Maslow's hierarchy of needs 24–25, 108–109
maths 18, 31, 49, 61, 65
meditative activities *see* mindfulness in nature
Mehrabian, A. 55
mental health 2–4, 11, 41, 71–73; anxiety 60, 81, 84–85, 128; attention deficit and hyperactivity disorder (ADHD) 6; circles of support 73; as continuum 77; depression 60, 80–81, 127; five ways of wellbeing 96–97; gratitude 38; obsessive compulsive disorder (OCD) 88–89, 129; poor 76–77; quiz 81, 126; roleplays 77; scenarios 77, 125; stress 92–93, 94, 131
mind mapping 9; anxiety 128
mindful listening 15
mindfulness in nature 94–95; birdsong 56–57; body scan 95; finger tracing 95; grounding 15, 56, 57, 74, 94; haiku 74–75; STOP 94
motivation 2; fear and phobias 28

natural colours 26–27, 34, 110
nature calm jars 98–99
nature connection 6; A–Z of noticing nature 78–79; birds *see separate entry*; butterflies 68–69, 75, 124; gratitude scavenger hunt 38–39, 116; habitats 52–53, 79, 119; haiku 74–75; insects 30–31, 112; mindfulness in nature *see separate entry*; natural colours 26–27, 34, 110; nature calm jars 98–99; nature mandalas 86–87; nest building 82–83; sensory sit-spot 34–35, 115; sonic sit-spot 14–15, 79, 94, 104; sustainability, signs of 60–61, 120; texture bingo 38, 39–40, 117; wildflowers 64–65, 123
nature deficit disorder (NDD) 5
nature mandalas 86–87
nature table 27, 39; sensory 45
needs, Maslow's hierarchy of 24–25, 108–109
nest building 82–83
noticing nature, A–Z of 78–79

obsessive compulsive disorder (OCD) 88–89; myths 89, 129
OFSTED (Office for Standards in Education, Children's Services and Skills) 4, 6, 11

phobias and fear 28–29, 111
place, sense of 48–49

poetry: haiku 74–75
Public Health England 2–3

reciprocity 11, 62, 66
relationships 2, 41; communication 54–55; fear and phobias 28; friendships 66–67, 81
resilience 4
respect 62–63, 121–122
roleplays 77
RSPB Big Schools' Birdwatch 19

safety net 63
SEAL (Social and Emotional Aspects of Learning) framework 2
self-awareness 2, 41, 42–43; fear and phobias 28; feelings 12; flower of awareness 43; happiness 36; SWOT analysis 58; triggers 16–17
self-care and coping 20–21; anger 32, 33; happiness 36
self-esteem 6, 81
self-regulation 2, 3, 94–95; calm jars 98–99; escalation curve 17, 105; fear and phobias 28; feelings 12; triggers 16–17
sensory sit-spot 34–35, 115
sit-spot: bird sounds 57; habitats 53; sensory 34–35, 115; sonic 14–15, 79, 94, 104
slideshow 9
social media 42, 50, 92
sonar map 15, 56, 57, 104
sonic sit-spot 14–15, 79, 94, 104
spotting sheets 79; birds 106; insects 112; wildflowers 123
stationery, general 9
statutory requirements 2, 3, 76
stigma 3, 80
street work: sense of place 48–49
stress 92–93, 94, 131
support, circles of 73
sustainability, signs of 60–61, 120
SWOT (strengths, weaknesses, opportunities, and threats) analysis 58–59

texture bingo 38, 39–40, 117
triggers 16–17
trust 62

website XenoCanto: bird sounds 56
wildflowers: identify and count 64–65, 123; spotting sheet 123
Wildfowl and Wetland Trust (WWT) 22
word starter 9

For Product Safety Concerns and Information please contact our EU representative GPSR@taylorandfrancis.com
Taylor & Francis Verlag GmbH, Kaufingerstraße 24, 80331 München, Germany

www.ingramcontent.com/pod-product-compliance
Lightning Source LLC
Chambersburg PA
CBHW082014220426
43670CB00015B/2624